INSPIRED LIVING

A GUIDE TO IGNITE JOY AND PROSPERITY

Concept: Krystal Hille
Editor: Jhenim Chai Carrascoso
Cover Design: Stephanie Wicker-Campbell (Muse Design)
Formatting: Shahid Aziz
Publishing: Hille House Publishing

Disclaimer:

The authors in this book do not dispense medical advice or prescribe the use of any technique as a form of treatment for physical, emotional, or medical problems without the advice of a physician, either directly or indirectly. The intent of the authors is only to offer information of general nature to help you in your quest for emotional, physical, and spiritual well-being. In the event you use any of the information in this book for yourself, the authors and the publisher assume no responsibility for your actions.

CONTENTS

PART-IV - IGNITING JOY

PART-V - WELCOMING PROSPERITY

INTRODUCTION

Inspiration is something we are born with, yet over time, conditioning, domestication, and fear can shut it down. Reclaiming inspiration and living an inspired life is something we all yearn for, whether we consciously dare to claim it or not.

Inspiration is a vibrational energy that can't connect with us when we are in survival mode, exhausted, or don't believe that we are worthy to fulfil our dreams. It visits us in the stillness, in the shower, and in nature. From the spark of inspiration and the inception of an idea, we have the potential to create a life of joy and prosperity. But this potential can only manifest when we truly believe that we are worthy of creating it.

The origin of the word inspiration in both Latin and old French means to inhale and breathe life into. In Middle English the word was used in the context of putting life or spirit into the human body. The Cambridge Dictionary defines inspiration as 'someone or something that gives you ideas for doing something... a sudden good idea'.

Who is this someone or something? Where do these sudden good ideas come from?

I believe they come from the divine, from the universal field of consciousness, from Source, Spirit, or whatever you wish to call it; they come from living 'in-spirit', from being a part of the All that Is, when we are tapped in, connected, and whole.

Do you believe that you are whole? Do you believe that you deserve to be connected and tapped into universal abundance? Do you believe that you are worthy to act on the inspired thoughts that 'Spirit' presents you?

The problem is that most of us don't. Not at first, anyway. So, we embark on this often-intense journey of trials and tribulations until we've finally had enough. That's when we start to ask different questions. Instead of the inner victim's voice: 'Why me?', we find our inner hero and heroine who recognise that they have choice and power. They ask: 'What needs to shift? How can I change? What help do I need?' These new questions open new dialogues that present new opportunities.

Living an inspired life means that we put ourselves first. It means that we value ourselves enough to feel that we deserve to be happy, joyous, and prosperous and allow ourselves time for self-care and silence where we can release beliefs that keep us small and in separation.

We are all children of the divine. We are all part of this magical universe. We are all one with nature. Let's remember these truths with every fibre of our being!

This book is structured into five sections that create a powerful journey of how to reclaim joy and prosperity in your life.

First, we must *Uncover Inspiration*, and I am honoured that Dr. Larry Farwell has contributed his extensive research on the science of miracles to this book. In his chapter, he demonstrates the scientific evidence of how we can all manifest miracles and live an inspired life.

Next, we explore how listening to our inspiration and *Following the Flow* brings greater ease into our lives.

Then, in *Unleashing Creativity*, we discover how creative expression can tap us deeper into the essence of who we are and thus opens us up to an inspired life.

In the section *Igniting Joy*, the contributors explore how we can make joy an active inquiry and how the focus on joy has enabled them to keep returning to inspiration.

Welcoming Prosperity is our final section. When we live in alignment with our true nature and embody the knowing that we are whole, we will return to universal abundance. Are you actually open to receiving? Are you ready to welcome all the blessings the universe has in store for you? It can feel overwhelming at times, and we need to get acclimated step by step. Otherwise, just like most lottery winners, we will lose our prosperity because we haven't yet learned to hold it energetically. Prosperity, just like inspiration and joy, are our birthright; all we need to do, is open to it fully.

Are you ready?

Meet the thought leaders who have each embarked on this journey into alignment, self-belief, and inspired living. Be moved by their stories and inspired to use their tools, so that you too, can step towards an inspired life of joy and prosperity.

Here is to living an inspired life and bringing more joy and prosperity into the world, so that we can all thrive at our highest potential.

With love,

Krystal

PART I

UNCOVERING INSPIRATION

DR. LARRY FARWELL

CURIOSITY AS A SUPERPOWER

UNLEASHING INSPIRATION TO CREATE MIRACLES AND LIVE A FULFILLED LIFE

*A*s a child, I was always curious about everything. I wanted to explore and understand everything, and fortunately for me, my father was a scientist. He was a physicist, and I asked him about everything. I wanted to understand not only how the physical world works but also what life is about, what we are here for, and why I am experiencing life the way I am.

I had some subtle perceptions ever since I was a baby, and so I was always wondering about the subtle energies of life, as well as the mechanics of how life works. I was also wondering, what are we here for, and how do we live fulfillment in your lives? I remember thinking about this even as a little kid: what makes life fulfilling? What creates a life that's worth being here for?

This inquiry got highlighted when I was 13 years old and almost drowned. I had a very profound transmutation experience. I got to the point where I thought I only had a few seconds to live, and several things happened all at once. One is that my life flashed before my eyes. I've heard those words before, but in this case, it was like everything was there all at once, as clear as waking life but all at once. I'd never had that experience of expanded consciousness before.

Another interesting thing happened. You know those situations in life that don't quite go the way you want them to go, where you think, "One day, maybe I'll go back and fix that." Even when something happened long ago that you are realistically never going to change. I still have that subtle feeling that I can always go back and fix things. In that moment, I realized that's never going to happen. I had to let go of everything. And as I let go of everything in my life, my experience completely shifted of what my life was. I felt that I saw my life for the first time as if I'd woken up from a dream. I saw it as completely perfect. It was what it was. It's not that I didn't see the mistakes or the pain, but it was completely perfect, and I had no regrets at all that I was only 13 years old. In that moment I felt as if everything was in the hands of nature and I had let go of everything.

Then my awareness came back to what I had been before, and I was back choking water and coughing and spitting. From that moment onwards, I knew that there was more to life than I'd ever imagined. And if I could get to that experience where I was embodying the real life, I would be able to live a life of fulfillment, a life that was meaningful to me and that expressed what I was here for.

I tried everything to recreate this expanded awareness. Over the next six years or so, I read all the books, took all the courses, and did all the meditations. I did everything because I knew there was more to life than I had experienced. I was trying to get to that state of enlightenment, and by the time I was in college, I really thought I was sort of an expert on those kinds of higher human developments. In reality, I was at the pre-kindergarten stage, but I didn't know that then.

I met Maharishi Mahesh Yogi when I was a student at Harvard. He is the founder of Transcendental Meditation, who came there to speak. I learned Transcendental Meditation from him and realized that in the field of pure consciousness, which is the essential constituent of life, who we really are at our essence... all of the great spiritual traditions teach us that this is the same as what we now call the conscious unified field. The unified field from which the particle-wave phenomena of quantum mechanics of nature spring from. In quantum-mechanical terms, the entire universe consists of patterns of vibration in the unified field. These appear as particles or as waves depending on how they are measured. Thus, the building blocks of the physical universe can be referred to as "particle-wave phenomena."

Learning Transcendental Meditation, I started to be able to experience this phenomenon within myself and gain some understanding of how it relates to life. I became curious about how we can tie that in with science since I grew up in a very scientific family. From the time I was a little kid, I did my own scientific experiments and always wanted to understand things and gain scientific clarity. And yet I knew that the unbounded realm of life was beyond what science had touched on. So as a neuroscientist, I started working on that with my dad, who is a physicist.

We decided to see if we could design an experiment to firstly find out if it is really the case that the inner field of pure conscience is the same as the unified field that quantum particle-wave phenomena spring from.

And perhaps even more vital to life than that, what can we do about it? If the inner field of pure consciousness which is our essential essence as conscious beings is the same as the unified field from which the physical universe springs like waves on an ocean, then it stands to reason that functioning from a high level of consciousness from within ourselves, we could create an effect in the physical world. We decided to test this. If we could have an effect on the physical world, using consciousness alone, without any physical intervention, this would be miraculous. So our investigation into the relationship of consciousness with the physical world – the real physical world, the world of quantum mechanics – would also be an investigation into the phenomenon of miracles. We set out to investigate scientifically what is a miracle, and how can we create miracles?

Can we create Miracles?

First of all, I had to come up with a clear scientific explanation of what a miracle is. I remember talking to my dad. I said: "Dad, anything is possible, right?" We were sitting at lunch in a restaurant. He said, "Yes, son, any imaginable configuration of quantum particle-wave phenomena is possible. Some are probable, some are improbable, and some are extremely improbable. But anything's possible." I continued my train of thought: "So it's possible then that you and I, all the particles that make up our bodies, and enough air to breathe, can tunnel from here to the other side of the moon, and we'll carry our conversation on there?" The tunnelling is a known phenomenon in quantum mechanics, which actually happens and is a finite probability. He said, "Yeah. In fact, that is possible." Then he got out a paper napkin and made some quick computations. He wrote out a formula that I still have and calculated the approximate probability that this scenario would happen. The probability was low, in fact it didn't happen, and we stayed right there in the restaurant. But the point is that we're talking science! We're not talking woo-woo here, nor are we talking about belief or mysticism. We're talking science, quantum mechanics, and what we can measure in a physics laboratory.

Any imaginable phenomenon is possible, no matter how improbable it seems. Some things are extremely improbable, but anything is possible! So then the question becomes, can we call a miracle simply an improbable event? We used to think that miracles contradict the laws of nature. Well, in quantum mechanics, anything's possible. A miracle is simply a highly improbable event. So we asked the question, can we create miracles? Can we create these highly improbable events?

We've all had an experience, I'm sure you have, too, where you think: "I'd really like to hear from Jennie" and moments later, the phone rings and it's Jennie. You wonder whether your consciousness had an effect on nature somehow. But you don't know the probability. Maybe Jennie would have called anyway. So that's not really a scientific experiment.

We've all had enough of such experiences that we think that maybe there's something there. But we don't know the probability. However, we do know the exact probability distribution of alpha particle emission by plutonium. This means that we can measure it and observe if it can deviate through the power of human thought. So we set up an experiment to see if we could create a shift in that probability distribution.

Plutonium is one of the major ingredients of an atomic bomb. My dad, when he was still a grad student, was on the Manhattan Project when he invented atomic energy and developed that first pump. Together, we set up an experiment. I did the neuroscience part, and he did the physics part using a standard nuclear physics apparatus.

The question we were asking is: can we create an extremely improbable event? I could go into the exact set-up and math, and I have done so in the physics journals, which you can look into if you are interested, but the short answer is, yes, we could! We were able to consciously shift the probability distribution of quantum mechanical events in one direction or another through pure intention. And then, we had a control condition where we didn't have any intention, and the particles stayed the same. What we showed is that human consciousness can create an extremely improbable event, which scientifically proved we can create miracles.

Applying our Consciousness

From all those wise and brilliant people throughout the ages who explained 'Here's how life works', along with all the Scriptures from two- or five- or ten thousand years ago, right down to the expert who wrote a book about success last week, they all say the same thing: you create a vision on the level of your consciousness, you enliven nature in that vision. You enliven what we now call the conscious unified field in that vision that sets up a vibration in nature, which in turn shows up in the world.

I play guitar and I sing. So if I pick up a guitar and pluck a guitar string, it'll vibrate at a particular resonant frequency. If there's another instrument in the environment that has a similar resonant frequency, it'll start to vibrate too. So if you set up that resonant frequency on the level of your awareness - and remember, your consciousness *is* that unbounded field that the universe springs from- you set up that vibration on that level, you enliven nature in that vibration, and then that shows up in the world.

All the wise people throughout the ages have said that, and what we showed in the laboratory is that that's how nature works. That's the mechanics of nature. And again, we are not talking woo-woo here. We showed in the laboratory that you enliven that desire at the level of your consciousness, and with no physical intervention, you can change the probability distribution of quantum mechanical events that are mathematically extremely improbable and off the charts in the statistics books. So what that means is we can create miracles, and it's simply a matter of applying our consciousness.

It is now 20 years ago since we did this research. I published a very technical, scientific book about our discovery along with publications in numerous scientific journals, and we also presented our findings at the American Physical Society. For the next 20 years, I've developed techniques to apply our consciousness so that we can create miracles in our lives. I have published these in my recent book: *The Science of Creating Miracles: Neuroscience, Quantum Physics and Living the Life of Your Dreams*.

It's about applying your consciousness to create the life of your dreams. Many people do this intuitively and what we have shown is that there's a scientific foundation for this. I've then developed techniques to apply that science to creating miracles in your life. So that's what my work now is about, and I had a sense of this as a young child. I knew that I wasn't just here to play in the woods. I wasn't just here to do impressive things and to have achievements. I was here to get a sense of what life was and to get a crystal-clear vision of that, demonstrate it and then apply it, so it's useful for other people as well.

Inspiration, Effortlessness, and Miracles

One of the things to keep in mind is that the way we contact the most powerful level of our *self*, the most powerful level of consciousness, is on the level of quietness, on the level of calmness, on the level of silence. The conscious unified field, our essential nature, our unbound conscious, it's quiet, it's silent, and subtle. So trying harder keeps your awareness on the surface. It doesn't allow you to tune into that subtle level of your own awareness to enliven the conscious unified field. Effortlessness is actually really a key to creating miracles in your life. Having that inner vision but not pushing that inner vision, having it, and letting it go.

My first revelation about letting go was when I was drowning. I let go of everything, and that was what opened my awareness. So opening the awareness to a higher level of consciousness is on a level of effortlessness; it's on the level of attunement with nature. The intellect and the emotions both function on an active level of the mind. The intuition is quieter. Tuning in to nature intuitively involves a subtle, quiet level of awareness. The intellect shouts; the emotions scream; the intuition whispers. Of course, being a scientist, I like the intellect. But the way you attune to nature, the way you figure out what nature is doing, and the way you command nature is on the level of your intuition, on the level of silently tuning into nature. Once that's established, you use the intellect as a tool to systematize it, prove it, and communicate it to others.

Inspiration takes place on the level of intuition, on the quieter level of the awareness. Inspiration literally means breathing in. As you breathe in, your awareness naturally tends to expand; you become more awake and aware. Inspiration is breathing in an attunement with Nature, and experiencing the enlivening effect that this has on your consciousness. It takes place on the level of quietness and intuition.

How to bring more inspiration into our lives, change our blueprint, and return to the *real* Self

Moving from physics to neuroscience, we can take advantage of the way the brain works. And this also has everything to do with inspiration and how we're bringing it into our lives.

You're crawling around the floor. You're two years old. You touch the floor, you touch the table leg, you touch the wall. You don't learn much from that, that you didn't already know. But when you touch the hot stove, you have an 'aha' experience that wakes you up and brings you flying into the present. This 'aha' opens your awareness up to reprogramming because now something important has come along that's going to make a difference in your life.

This 'aha' experience is something that I've studied a lot as a neuroscientist. I discovered that when you have an 'aha' experience, it opens your brain up for reprogramming. An 'aha' experience has a corresponding phenomenon that takes place in your brain function. This is called memory and encoding related multifaceted electroencephalographic response, M-E-R-M-E-R, in short, a MERMER. I've spent a large part of my career investigating this P300-MERMER, this "Aha!" experience.

A couple of my major inventions, including brain fingerprinting, have involved applying this phenomenon that can be picked up in the brain. We can measure the brainwaves of what is happening when someone has an 'aha' experience. I'll bet anything that when Buddha attained enlightenment, he had an 'aha' moment. I bet if we had had brainwave measurements going on, we would have seen this P300-MERMER in his brainwaves.

So when something really gets your attention, when something really gets to you, you have this 'aha' experience, and it opens your mind and your brain up for reprogramming.

Now let's look at what happens in our life. We go around, and things are pretty normal, and then something comes along that really makes an impact. This can be a very positive experience, but let's talk about the experiences we usually try to avoid. When something comes along someone does or says something that seems to be damaging or threatening to us, it usually threatens our value, safety, or power. How do those experiences of value, safety, and power come about? Well, we create within us an inner blueprint that we are only say 75% valuable, 64% powerful, and 83% safe. So then we resonate with that, nature also resonates with that, and look: we get all of this evidence coming at us, 'objective' evidence from outside, proving that we're *not* 100% valuable, and only 75% powerful, and 64% safe, or whatever it is.

The truth is that this unbounded, conscious unified field creates a whole universe where you're infinitely valued, 100% safe, and 100% powerful. But we're carrying around a blueprint that's less than that. So every once in a while, we get an experience that seems to be a challenge to our value, safety, or power. When someone says or does something that triggers us, we have a choice. We can choose an inspired choice or a less inspired choice. We can choose to shoot and punish the messenger and externalize the experience, or we can internalize it and tell ourselves that "maybe I really am a horrible person." We can get depressed, frightened, anxious, or whatever.

Now here's the take-home message: when something comes along that triggers you and gives you an 'aha' experience or MERMER moment, your brain opens up for reprogramming. Instead of reacting, tune into who you *really* are, tuned into reality. Let the awareness settle down. Let the awareness go inward and get a feeling, a sense, a holographic experience of the *real* you: 100% safe, 100% valuable, 100% powerful. Not that you're sitting there saying those words to yourself, although that can be a starting point. You tune into that level of your life that is unbound, pure consciousness, and the conscious unified field of your own essence. You tune into yourself and enliven that reality. That's when you can tune into the *real* you and have the experience that you are 100% safe, 100% valuable, and 100% powerful. This then creates a shift in your blueprint and is what we call transmutation.

Transmutation versus Transformation

There's a lot of talk about transformation, where you transform and change the form of something where you transform your thoughts, your emotions, your beliefs, your attitudes, and so on. Transmutation is a shift in who is creating those thoughts. It's a shift that takes place on the level of your being, and it comes from tuning into the reality of who you are.

So as a practical matter, when something comes along that triggers you, use it as a trigger for transmutation. We call it a transmutation trigger. Instead of reacting, tune in to who you *really* are and use that as a trigger to reprogram your brain in order to experience more and more of your true blueprint: 100% safe, 100% valuable, 100% powerful. Then you start aligning this blueprint nature and it shows up in your world.

Now you can turn these experiences you've been trying to avoid upside down. When someone comes along and triggers you, you can start to smile because you realize that this is an opportunity. You can tell yourself: this is not something to avoid because it is opening my brain up for reprogramming at the level of my essence so that I can start to live more of my *real* life. That's sort of what happened to me when I was 13 years old. It really got my attention and when I let go of everything, it allowed me to tune into more of the reality of my life.

We don't have to wait for near-death experiences; we can create them at will. And just to add: MERMER experiences can also be really positive. Yes, it can mean touching a hot stove for the first time, but it can also be created by touching somebody that you are extremely attracted to in a loving way. In either case, you can use those as triggers for transmutation, for the unfolding of your own being and the *real* you.

I believe that this is what we are here to do. We're here to transmute our experience of life from one of limitation to one of unboundedness, from one of suffering to one of fulfillment, and from one of limitation to one of inspiration. Inspiration literally means 'breathing in'. You are breathing in who you *really* are. You're breathing in all of nature. You're opening yourself up to your own full value and up to the full value of nature, the conscious unified field that gives rise to all of creation.

If you look deeply enough, what's really going on in the physical universe when you go to the molecular level, the atomic level, the subatomic level, down to the subatomic particles, down to the string theory level, what you see as the physical universe, is just vibrating strings; vibrations, perturbations in the conscious unified field.

The whole physical universe is simply vibrations in that conscious unified field; that is who you are. This explains why we have such an intimate relationship with nature and with each other because, at the fundamental level, it's all one. And when we tune into that level, we can function from the most powerful level within nature.

So to conclude, the key to creating an inspired life is to know yourself, be yourself, and love yourself. This comes from tuning in to the *real you* within. And to know you is to love you. So as you know yourself, as you *be* yourself, you're bound to love yourself. And when you love yourself, everyone else will follow suit. They will pick up on that love, and you will find yourself surrounded by the love you're creating in your own life. When you know yourself, be yourself, and love yourself, you will be spontaneously living in harmony with your own nature, and with all of Nature. This enlivens your true self along with the almighty power of Nature in your life, bringing success and fulfillment on every level..

ABOUT THE AUTHOR

DR. LARRY FARWELL

DR LARRY FARWELL is the world's leading expert on the Science of Creating Miracles. He is the author of the #1 bestselling book *The Science of Creating Miracles: Neuroscience, Quantum Physics, and Living the Life of Your Dreams* and was selected by *TIME* magazine as one of the TIME 100 Top Innovators of the Century, "The Picassos or Einsteins of the 21st Century". He is also the inventor of the first Brain-Computer Interface and Brain Fingerprinting.

As a Harvard-educated neuroscientist, Dr. Larry Farwell's revolutionary scientific research in neuroscience, quantum physics, and the role of consciousness in life and the universe has introduced a new scientific paradigm. He has developed practical techniques to apply the Science of Creating Miracles in life.

Dr. Farwell has worked with individuals, governments, agencies, high-ranking officials including heads of state, leaders, and organizations throughout the world, including the President of the United States, the US Navy, the FBI, the CIA, and their counterparts around the world. He has published his research in the leading peer-reviewed scientific journals. He has been featured in major news media worldwide.

Connect with Dr. Larry Farwell to find out about his online workshops, video courses, and more.

Website: https://drlarryfarwell.com/

SYLVIA MORRISON

QUANTUM LEAP

READY OR NOT, HERE I COME!

*M*ost people believe that in order to create the change that they want to see or experience, they need to have done extensive research and have a well-laid-out plan before they begin. The exceptional reality that I have experienced throughout my life is that: by taking inspired action, I tap into the limitlessness of my power.

I have accomplished some big hairy audacious goals that would have scared me half to death or stopped me in my tracks if I had them all planned out. I take inspired action, and I experience the unconditional support of the Source of All that Is.

Inspired living is a life of Trusting that the Mastermind of this whole universe supports my journey and has my back. To live an inspired life, I listen to my intuition and act on its messages. When I feel fear creeping in, I return to stillness and communion with the power that lives within me. I believe that Life is always seeking to express its brilliance and creativity through each of us. So whenever I feel inspired by an idea, I remind myself that whatever is required to manifest the idea will arrive in the same way that the idea did.

It was 2019 when I gave up my teaching and consulting career in Canada, sold my house, packed up life, and moved to Ghana, West Africa. All of which I had not planned.

It was a beautiful winter morning in February. I liked the feeling of the crisp fresh air on my face and was fascinated by the patterns that appeared when the warm air exhaled from my nostrils touched the cold air of winter. I was on my way to work, teaching at the college in Toronto, and as I crossed the street, something inside me suddenly said, *make this your last winter.* A feeling of joy welled up inside me. It was as if I had just received the beautiful surprise of a desired gift. I thought, "wow, I would certainly love that!"

The bus arrived, and as soon as I got my seat, I quickly sent a text message to my daughter; "Guess what, honey, this will be my last winter in Canada!"

The thought would pass through my mind throughout the day, and a feeling of joy would swell throughout my being. I didn't think of how this would be possible, but I knew that I would genuinely love it if it happened.

About three weeks later, while reading and grading my students' essays and exams, the same voice said to me, "sell the house." I began daydreaming about the possibilities, and two hours later, I called a realtor and invited her over for a conversation to discuss the house selling process.

This was the last week of February, and I would be travelling for *Links Across Borders* annual library building trip to Ghana with volunteers in May, three months later. I told my realtor that *I would love it* if she would list the house on the day I would depart to Ghana and have it sold by the time I returned three months later. She assured me that she would try her best. She also warned me that it would require significant effort on my edge to get the house organized and ready for Showing in a few weeks. I thought about it and began to wonder how I would make it happen. *It seemed almost impossible.*

In addition to my involvement with various community projects in my city, and my coaching practice, I was teaching three courses to 150 college students that semester. That involved a great deal of marking essays and exams, submitting grades, student consultations, and staff meetings. I was definitely not ready to prepare a four-bedroom house for a successful show and sale. I felt fear creeping in...Am I biting off more than I could chew?

"Are you sure you are ready for this move, Sylvia?" she asked. I asked her about the alternative; she explained. If I prepared the house after returning from Ghana at the end of July, it would be less stressful. Without school on my calendar, I would have lots of time on my hands. It sounded much more manageable and would give me more lead time, but I did not love the idea. We agreed that she would visit in a couple of days and show me exactly what needed to be done to prepare the property for sale.

On the day she returned, after listening to her outline the required; packing, renovations, and cleaning involved, I told her that it sounded scary, and I did not feel ready but would do it. In the weeks that followed, my body was constantly filled with the intensity of feelings; fear and excitement. Sometimes I would lay awake wondering what the hell have I done. Other times, I could hardly contain the excitement of moving to Ghana and living the dream that I had held in my heart for so many years.

I wanted to give the children in Ghana what the library in my village gave me when I was a child. Books opened the world beyond my neighbourhood and caused me to dream, imagine, and experience life that was different than the realities in my surroundings. I traveled the world through books. I wanted to give that to the children in rural Ghana.

I had the house ready for the market in a few weeks. As I was leaving for the airport on May 4th, my realtor placed the 'For Sale' sign on my lawn. I said yes to the idea that I was in love with—and through taking inspired actions— I succeeded. And by June 31, my house was sold.

I returned at the end of July, and the Sale sign was on my lawn. The sale will close on August 31. I now had one month to pack and move all my belongings, but I had not found a place to go. I had no intentions of buying another house. I was leaving Canada to live in Ghana. Where would I live in the meantime? What would I do with my full garage of *Links Across Borders* books and school supplies that I had stored for shipment to Ghana? What household items would I keep, give, or throw away?

I was NOT ready. During the four weeks of August, especially Moving Day, my life felt scary. I wasn't prepared, but Spirit sent me helpers throughout the day to facilitate the process and support me at every turn. It was unbelievable how everything worked out. To top it off, at the end of the day, my lawyer waited for me at her office until late evening to give me the cheque. This was way more than I would have asked.

It is my hope that reading this chapter encourages you to ACT on your inspiration so that you can live the life of Fulfilment and Freedom that you desire and deserve.

Assess and Acknowledge your current life. What's stirring in your heart, soul?

What keeps you awake, feeling anxious, or worried at night? Your discontent.

What delights you—that it fills your heart with joy just by the mere thought of it or seeing someone doing it? Your desire.

Connect and Claim the truth that you are a Spiritual being having a human experience. Life is seeking a fuller, more delightful expression of itself through you *and* by means of you. Connect with the desire or deep longing that is in your heart to change your life, and make a difference in the lives of many others. You are connected to the limitless supply of ALL that is. Claim your power to be, do, give, and have the life you feel inspired to live.

Tap in and Touch the thing to which you are feeling Called. You CAN begin it today by taking action you feel heart-inspired to take. Do what you can, where you are, with what you already have.

We each have the power to live by designing a life that is revitalizing, invigorating, and fulfilling.

I said yes to the idea that I was in love with and took inspired actions.

In my work with clients, I guide them in choosing to no longer live by default, following the expectations of others along the predictable path while ignoring the ever-present feeling of discontent. I teach them to ask empowering questions to help them access the answers needed to choose Inspired Living. Here are five questions that could help you:

1. What Would I Love?

2. Will It Cause Me to Grow?

3. Is There Good In It For Others?

4. Will I Need Help From A Higher Power?

5. What Action Can I Take, Where I Am, With What I Have?

Building Libraries in Ghana

I am the Founder of *Links Across Borders*. For the past nine years we've been building libraries and coordinating International Service Abroad opportunities for students and individuals who desire to make an impact while having fun. This continues to be my journey of Inspired Living.

I did not know what would be required to create the first library. In my travels to various Ghanaian villages, it had occurred to me that children didn't have access to books, and I had not seen libraries in their villages. I was born and raised in a rural community in Jamaica. My family couldn't afford lots of books, but there was a library in my community. Having access to books helped me dream and imagine a life more extensive than I saw in my neighbourhood. I had a desire for the children in rural Ghana to have libraries, but I thought someone with access to the financial resources and knowledge required should do something about that.

I was surprised in May 2012 when I heard myself say out loud, at a community meeting, that I would build a library in 2013. I did not have a plan, but I had a desire in my heart to provide children in Ghana with access to books. Spirit knew that the desire was in my heart and decided to give voice to it in that meeting. When the idea popped into my consciousness, I was elated. It felt like I had completed the library, and I was proud, grateful, and delighted.

One year later, in collaboration with a beneficiary community, the first library was completed. At the Opening Ceremony event, with hundreds of people gathered, I heard myself announce that I would create libraries all over Ghana. The audience erupted in dance and applause. I, simultaneously, was frightened and delighted.

By taking one inspired action after another, *Links Across Borders* completed eight libraries in 7 years and has facilitated Volunteer Abroad experiences for over 200 individuals and groups between 2013 to 2019.

The Volunteer Abroad program started without a plan in place. It was the first day of the Fall semester of 2012; My new students were introducing themselves by responding to 3 questions. One question was: What would you do if you had a million dollars now? When it was my turn to respond, I said I would use a portion of that money to build libraries in Ghana and offer

International Student Placements as of 2013. To my astonishment, a student raised her hand and announced that she would love to go. I *swallowed my tongue* when she asked how she could apply. I kept my composure and promised to speak with her after class. Although deep down, I was hoping that she would forget about it in 3 hours. But no. She didn't.

I had to come up with a plan by the end of class. I didn't have the entire plan, but I had the first action. "Send me your resumè." She sent it, and within two weeks, ten students sent me their resumès. Only one of those students was in any of my classes. The others heard about this opportunity from the one student who was beyond excited that she now had her first-year placement in Ghana. On May 7th, 2013, I boarded a flight to Ghana with my first Group: 16 individuals who were realizing their dream of travelling to Ghana. We spent three weeks in Ghana, completed the first library, and that year I was enstooled as Queen Mother in this village.

None of this would have happened had I not acted on the inspiration to build a library-and offer the International Placement. Inspired Living allows me to fulfil desires that seemed impossible.

I live an Inspired life by trusting my Intuition, believing that the power to create is within me, and by taking the best possible action available at the moment. You can do this too. When I feel inspired, and doubt tries to creep in, I ask myself the five questions that I offered earlier in this chapter. If my answers are YES, then I'm assured that the desire or idea is right for me, so I trust my Intuition and take inspired actions.

I would be happy to support you in living your Inspired Life in harmony with your soul. Connect with me for a FREE 30-minute Activation Session. In this guided session, you will:

ACKNOWLEDGE What's stirring in your heart.

CONNECT to the limitless supply of Source; your power to be, do, give, and live in harmony.

TOUCH the thing to which you are feeling called, by taking the action you feel heart-inspired to take.

You deserve to live the life of your dreams. Welcome to the journey of Inspired Living!

ABOUT THE AUTHOR

SYLVIA MORRISON

SYLVIA MORRISON is a humanitarian and founder of *Links Across Borders*, a non-profit organization that co-creates libraries in Ghana, West Africa.

Ms. Morrison, an educator, taught at George Brown College and appeared on Rogers TV and CBC Radio in Toronto, Canada. She worked extensively in the area of gender-based violence; as a counselor/advocate for women survivors of trauma and sexual assault.

As an Empowerment Specialist, Sylvia teaches transformational principles through coaching, keynotes, and retreats internationally. She believes that when we begin to tune into our intuition and become aware of our connection with Source Power, we can move from fear of the unknown to love and trust; a state in which we take inspired action.

Ms. Morrison facilitates a reliable five-step process that moves clients and audiences from overwhelmed and stuck, to being clear, energized, and inspired to ACT, bringing their unique gift to the world.

Sylvia enjoys a life of freedom and flexibility while making an everlasting difference in the lives of children in Ghana, West Africa.

Connect with Sylvia here:

Website: https://sylviamorrison.com/

Freebie: Claim your free A.C.T. connection call here: me@sylviamorrison.com

To learn more and support *Links Across Borders* visit https://linksacrossborders.org

RANDY BROWN

MUSIC: MY EVER-PRESENT FRIEND

*W*aiting by the front door for me was my yellow Sony Walkman loaded with a very special cassette tape. At the same time, every day that winter and spring, I would head west down Orchard Dr. walking slowly at first but eventually at a frantic pace. My destination was Main Street, where I would cross the street and wind through the curvy path through Dry Run Creek for as far as I could go.

Turning around, I would walk the same steps in the opposite direction to get me home. My feet were in Cedar Falls, Iowa, but not my head. I'm not one for soft music. I'm into the blaring variety of guitar-driven rock n roll. On this day, I listened to the same thing I had listened to many days before and would listen to for many days to come. Austin, TX-based blues guitarist, Chris Duarte, created the amazing guitar work that took me for a walk daily, sometimes twice a day. Songs like Big Legged Woman, My Way Down, Cleopatra, Scrawl, Letter from my Girlfriend, and Tailspin Headwhack were embedded into my brain. The same bootleg tape over and over and over. Somehow, this worked for me as those walks became something I could count on happening every day. It created some hope—maybe, within me— knowing that I could trust that the music would be present, uplift me, and never stop. Hope is one of the greatest gifts we have in life. It's when hope is illusive that we can give up on our lives.

Hope can be many things, but in this specific time of my life, it was the music that gave me hope. I didn't question it because I was too busy trusting it would be there the next day.

I understand this is not normal, but then in the state I was in during the spring of 1998, I had no idea what normal was. In February, we experienced the gut-wrenching death of our beautiful almost four year old daughter Natalie. I had fallen into a deep, cold, frightening place in the days and weeks that followed. A numbness enveloped me as my life was nothing more than a thick fog of indifference. To complicate the matter was the fact that six years prior, our firstborn, Meredith, also died of the same rare and rapidly acting disease. For months, all I remember about the day was walking this path and listening to the same songs by Chris. I had hit my rock bottom, and I remember thinking, "this is worse than I expected it to be." It was the lowest of my lows, and life seemed undoable at the time. It is in these moments in life we grasp for anything to lift us. My body felt like a thousand pounds when I was depressed; heavy, and lethargic. Just turning over from one side to the other was a monumental feat.

Have you ever been to a place like this? How did it feel to you? More importantly, where did you seek relief? Was it food, sunlight, television, movies, or a dark room?

Getting out of bed and using the bathroom was a chore, and showering was out of the question.

Food held no interest, nor did the news and even sports. Reading, puzzles, cleaning, and a hundred other daily chores didn't matter. I would always find the motivation to sit with my girls and watch a movie but usually fell asleep as soon as possible.

So, why was music the only thing that symbolized the idea that life might get better? Have you ever thought about it in that manner? If so, you may just find music a tool you can use throughout your life to pull you out of the inevitable holes we all slip into from time to time.

Looking back on those difficult and dark years, I can now see why music always held space for me. Music has always represented creativeness and skill, mixed with a dash of craziness and showmanship thrown in for good measure.

I believe that you have to be a little crazy or driven to be a musician. One day it hit me, and I realized why I had clung so tightly to the tunes of my life. It was simple, really. I listened to music basically at two times; one, to get me going when I needed a little kick in the butt or motivation to pop out of bed. It was a way to make me feel better and be in a happier state. Secondly, music was a common denominator during the times I was having a ball. When I think back on the gang of guys I hung out with in high school and college. Music was like oxygen; it was necessary for a good time! My buddy Kurt would exclaim at college parties that it was "too early for Petty". Meaning, things needed to ramp up before Tom Petty hit the speakers. When it was time for AC/DC's popular Back in Black, it was also time for my air guitar-wielding impersonation of lead guitarist Angus Young. These were traditions we hold sacred to this day. When I think back on those days, I always crack a smile. The tunes are always part of the scene, and the volume was healthy.

What does music represent to you?

Does it remind you of a person, place, or time in your life and make you smile?

Does it relax you and take your mind away from the daily minutiae?

Is music able to rescue you from a tough day at work or relationship struggle?

The answer may indicate that music does for you want it has done for me, too.

One thing I've always had plenty of in my life is an interest in many things. Call it passion, love, or desire to learn, observe, or do certain activities in life; it's all the same. I happen to use the words 'inspiration' or 'inspire.' Words like 'happy' or 'like' are lifeless words for me, probably because of their repetitive use. 'Inspire' is a word that elicits thoughts of wonderment, possibilities, excitement, goosebumps, tingles, butterflies in the stomach, and sheer amazement. When I think of inspiration, I think of watching Walt Disney shows as a kid. Everything about Disney screamed inspiration and transported me to another world. That was my childhood. Whether it was catching big largemouth bass, chipping the golf ball close to the hole, making my first basket in the driveway, hearing my first rock n roll record, or learning I could be anything and do anything I desired if I loved it enough and worked as hard as possible for it—I was inspired by it all.

Being involved in sports was natural due to my father's career as a sportswriter. The practices, games, winning, losing, and the write-up in the paper the next day were such big things to me, and I wanted to be a part of it. When I learned that involvement in sports, which I learned to love at an early age, was possible for me, I found it easy to daydream about the time when I was old enough to be a high school student and play for my local high school. When that became a reality, as a high school basketball player, I would count the stars on the flag during the National Anthem and timed it, so the last star coincided with the song's last note. During the song, I thought of being a kid and dreaming about being on that big stage playing in front of hundreds of fans. With my feet firmly on the floor, memories flashed in and out of my mind as a young guy growing up and playing every day because it was that important to him. Now it was a reality, and this ritual became my inspiration to put every ounce into playing for the Fort Dodge Dodgers. I was inspired and ready to go when the buzzer sounded to start the game.

Observation is also a tool I used to experience inspiration. Watching people in conversation is still an enjoyable experience. I like to watch the faces, body language, and expressions people have, whether talking or listening. When laughter strikes, it's amazing how a face becomes distorted, and a variety of sounds come forth. Have you ever observed people as they ride the train, wait in line, are caught in contemplation, or read? It can tell you a lot about what is really going on in the mind of people and can include every expression we are capable of. A fun exercise is studying the face of a person opening a gift. A range of faces is part of this experience, followed by gratitude, disappointment, or a holler for joy! When people are engaged in an activity that requires effort, such as walking, running, yelling, competing in a sport, or rushing to catch the bus. This is another opportunity to study body and facial expressions. When a game is decided literally at the buzzer, it is so heartfelt to study the language of the winning and losing teams. Instantly one team leaps off the floor, projecting sweat in all directions and yelling unknown phrases as the other slumps and displays a face that knows defeat all too well.

As I've observed my entire life, it's the inspired gestures and expressions that I seek out most. There is something magical about that look of astonishment and wonderment. Of both success and surprise. It's one I've been addicted to my entire life, and I look for it every day.

Some people spend their entire weekends putting together scrapbooks, while others watch sports or exercise. Some spend endless hours quilting while others attend classic car shows, geocaching, or baseball card collector events. Some are in their gardens, while others are in the basement or greenhouse. Others go fishing while others pick up litter in highway ditches. There are an infinite number of hobbies, but our DNA is filled with specific strains of interest that drive us to pursue them relentlessly. There is a website called "List of Hobbies; The Ultimate List of 1000+ Hobbies to Try," which I find fascinating. Mine is a long list of inspirations that have captured me over a lifetime.

To begin with, people are fascinating in general, along with laughter, goosebumps, kindness, compassion, friendship, turning misfortune into greatness, teaching, sharing, leadership, empathy, and love. Life is so inspiring if we just take a step back and appreciate it with an open heart, allowing ourselves to be taken up in the possibilities.

Music has provided me with the most inspiration of all my life experiences to date. Each day I learn more about the complexities of music, from its simplest form to highly complex classical manuscripts. The sounds, their cadence and timing, the volume, beat, and words can all come at once. It may appear overwhelming, yet it all delicately comes together to form the most beautiful songs or compositions. It could be bluegrass or country, or it may be classical, rock, or new age. It all has been carefully arranged, and when instruments and voices are added in just the right place and time, it can carry me off on a breeze. Nothing inspires me like music.

As a child, the senses can be overwhelming, but music's sound always captured me. It could be the soothing sound of elevator music, songs on the radio as I sped down the street, church music combined with human voices, celebrations, the pep band at basketball games, or the chime of the bells on the ice cream truck rounding the corner and getting closer and closer.

On February 4, 1964, I experienced one of my life's great moments—one that continues to drive my love for music. That's the night that the Beatles made their first US television appearance in front of 73 million people on the Ed Sullivan show. The hysteria that surrounded that black and white television show is undeniable. Ironically I took no interest in The Beatles that night as much as what the music "did" to people in that live audience and those watching around the world. The tears, reaching arms toward the band, and the screeching sounds of screaming girls left an impression. How could this music be so different and special that people would act so astonishingly different, albeit for a few minutes? Many have tried to explain what happened that night, but I'm not sure anyone has really nailed it. It was magic. That inspiration still drives me to this day.

Most of the music of my youth came from sharing a bedroom with my older brother, Rick, four years my senior. He was cool because he had albums and would play them constantly. He remembered hearing about a guy from Detroit by the name of Nugent. His band, The Amboy Dukes, was making a name for themselves in the early seventies. And by the time I began buying albums, they were ready to explode. My first live concert experience watching Ted Nugent in 1976 was beyond description. It was inspiration like I didn't know existed. He played with a wild, unbridled style of running the stage, jumping from speakers, screaming in the mic, and assaulting the crowd with the volume of a 747. In wonderment, I asked myself repeatedly, "what would possess a musician to be taken by his music to react like this?" So that has been a question I've pondered about people and life forever. It's a fascinating study of the human condition and the things that move them. As long as I'm alive to observe, I'll be intrigued.

So many things about music take me away. One of the things that may have kept me listening is the snowflake effect. Of all of the songs composed, recorded, practiced, and played, no two of them are identical. Just like a snowflake, each is uniquely created. Two people or two bands can play the same song on paper, but the result in pure music is not the same. Even if the same person records the same song twice, something in each of those cuts will make them unique. Every day more and more music is recorded and released. 97 million. That's the number of songs that have been created and are on record (on paper, not on record album). Spotify, for example, has 82 million tracks of music on its platform, and not two of them are the same. If you don't believe me, listen to them all and let me know if you found twins.

It won't happen. To me, that is utterly amazing, and it's one of the things that draws me to music.

What do all of these music stories have to do with inspiration?

First, I guess it means I really, really like music. Secondly, it creates motivation and memories of life's good times with music. Thirdly, it's not going away any time soon.

To be inspired is one thing. It can be for a minute or a lifetime. It can evaporate, or it can find its way into your core. What are the benefits of being inspired?

Appreciation, momentary highs, goosebumps, applause, hugging someone or doing something nice for them, or moving you to action. Being moved to action to help the human race is the most powerful example of inspiration in motion. And if the music does anything, it inspires that deep place within you and, if only for a moment, makes you feel better.

Deep down, I know what it all means. Music is a reflection of my desire to honor those in music from the first song ever written until today. Those who dreamed of being rock stars and those who did. It's those who sacrificed their musical careers in order to put food on the table and raise a family. This includes peering deeply into an artist's eyes to gauge their passion and unwavering drive to write the next big song, release the next album, or board the bus for the next tour. It's the worn faces impacted by the hundreds of thousands of miles of concrete highway, as well as the unsavory food and restrooms. It encompasses their divorces, spirit, addictions, disappointments, high water marks, endless travel, laughter, sadness, and riding the ever-changing landscape of the music industry. It covers all of the highs and countless lows faced in a career in music. It's for the look on the band's faces when they arrive at a venue with fewer than ten people in attendance. And honestly, those end up being some of the best shows ever because the artist's real love and passion for their craft come out like a lion— That says everything about both the musician and how important those songs, perfectly played, are to them. And what's it all for? A song! And a warm heart!

Music has run the course of my life. It's different now. Before, music was used to drive the pain away with the sheer volume and to exhibit my rebellious side. Now, it's not the fear I run from but the inspiration I seek and have been drawn to. As Kevn Kinney of Drivin' N' Cryin' once said, "Turn it up or turn it off, Ted."

ABOUT THE AUTHOR

RANDY BROWN

RANDY BROWN is an inspirational speaker, award winning author, and life coach. His experience spans over 30 years of sharing life-changing messages to hundreds of audiences. With the book, *Life, Business, and the Universe, Vol. 4*, he became an International Best-Selling author in 2021.

Randy's powerful and transparent platform, "The Rebound Effect," is changing lives. His rise in the basketball coaching world was matched by his dramatic plunge to the depths of depression, two daughter's deaths, prison, divorce, and a career lost forever. His "Five R" formula allows his clients to move from broken to brilliant, living a thriving heart-centered life. His book *Rebound Forward; Rebound from Life's Most Devastating Losses and Stay in the Game*, is a popular book for those wanting to overcome adversity in life.

His impressive resume as a college basketball coach includes five NCAA Tournaments, back-to-back Big 12 titles, and the 2000 Elite Eight. Twelve NBA players have benefitted from his coaching expertise, including Steve Kerr, current Golden State Warriors head coach.

Randy has daughters Claire, 30, and Jane, 25.

Connect with Randy here:

Website: http://rbspeaks.com

Free Offer: 30 minute "Rebound Effect" Strategy Session. To sign up, send email to rb@rbspeaks.com, subject line: Strategy Session.

Linktree: https://linktr.ee/rbspeaks

SIBA YAGHI

DEATH IN COLORS

How could you do this to me? You did not do it. You did not leave.

These were the words Selena repeated again and again when she got to know that her 29-year-old sister, Merida, had passed away. Merida was young, beautiful, full of life, and very energetic. So, how could she die? She had so much to give; she held a complete world in her heart. Her hazel eyes were full of words, music, of songs; looking in her eyes, one could see two beautiful planets full of love, compassion, and, most importantly, honesty and integrity.

Merida & Selena! Who are they? How were they raised? What bond did they hold? And how did Selena deal with the loss of her beloved sister? And was her death a real loss, or was it a messenger who came to free both sisters' souls?

Born and raised in Baalbeck, a beautiful historical city in the west valley of Bekaa, the two sisters had a caring woman who loved her children to the extent that she would do anything for them. Her family was her whole world; she wanted them educated as she believed that education and only education would be their gateway to leave the city where the jungle law is the ruler and the rich get richer, and the poor get poorer. However, she was struggling with a silent divorce for twenty years due to the differences in the couple's priorities. Merida and Selena shared an unbreakable bond. Their voices could be heard giggling out loud, keeping their other siblings awake at night.

They had the gift of finding a reason to laugh in every situation; they firmly believed that laughter could heal wounds. Even when their parents divorced, they could always find something to laugh about. Even when their parents got a divorce, they always found a reason to laugh. Hence, they were growing empty without their mother; Selena found that food was the only way to shut down the voices of fear, guilt, and shame. She was ashamed of her parents' divorce since "being divorced" in a middle eastern country meant that the whole family was substandard. The young girl was lost—disconnected from her own soul and unable to understand or deal with her emotions. She was overwhelmed; she felt that she was fifty when she was only twelve. Her only way to cold the fire in her heart and stomach was by overeating in a hysterical way. In six years, she succeeded in being the most obese young girl in the town, where she was heavily bullied. Selena showed up as a strong, smart, and funny young girl. Her peers loved and cherished her, and she had the highest degrees at school. But deep inside, she felt that she was everything but a female, that she was incomplete and inferior to her girlfriends. She embodied her shame with a great sense of humor where she was the one to make jokes about herself. She used to run away from the staring eyes to hide and cry in her own cocoon, which only Merida was allowed to enter. Merida was by her side the entire time, doing her best to erase the hurtful words.

Still, Selena wanted more. She wanted the whole world to say sorry for what she had gone through and to make sure this would never happen to her again. Merida could not help her as she gradually got away from her and stepped into a prison that she had built for herself. Distorted convictions were the solid walls of this dark jail. A deformed belief system was the hard ground on which she stood her feet. She tried to bury her caring, loving, and compassionate soul. She did not recognize that a soul would never be buried and that she could never shut off the light of her own spirit. While Merida did her best to stay focused and connected to her own calling, Selena was looking everywhere for distractions and shortcuts to feel numb. She so badly wanted recognition, success, and acceptance that she was ready to compromise her values for them. She could not say "no" to anyone or anything as she wanted to be loved by everybody. She did not care about how she felt; she only cared about how she looked. The two sisters were growing apart. Although they shared each other's journeys, Merida perceived Selena as a hypocrite who was living by double standards and who was lying to herself just to keep the show going. In contrast, Merida was very unrealistic and illogical in the eyes of Selena.

It was Sunday Morning when Selena's mom called crying: "Selena! Your sister is dying!!! Please go to her now. I need two hours to get to you!!!!

Selena was numb; for the first time in her life, she couldn't think of a plan!! "Dying!!!! My sister is dying!!! No. It can't be true. Death happens to other people. Not to me. Not to my family. No to my sister. Merida is ok. She hit the Gym on Friday. How could she be dying? There must be a mistake!!! I will go, check on her, call mom and tell her that everything is under control! When she first reached the hospital, she ran to the reception and asked for her sister's room. The receptionist's answer was very cold and illogical to her; "Sorry Mam, your sister is in intensive care. You can't go there as she might be Covid positive." Selena tried and tried, but the doctors refused to get her in. They calmed her down, saying: "Let us show you her medical tests. Your sister was infected by a virus. We really don't know where it came from; her medical state is getting worse with time. We are sorry, we did everything to save her, but her body is not responding. Merida is already dead; it's a matter of hours before she counts her last breaths".

The whole world felt too small for her—she was paralyzed, unable to talk, and her feet couldn't bear her. How could her young beautiful sister leave so early? There must be a mistake! She stood up and politely asked the doctor to see her sister's tests—which she forwarded to several other doctors in other hospitals—while she waited for one doctor to tell her that there was something she could do to save her beloved sister. Unfortunately, the answer was one: "It's a matter of time; the only thing you can do is to pray for her." "I want to see her," she begged with broken eyes. They refused. She walked out into the hospital waiting room, numb, confused, unconvinced with the doctors' explanation, and full of guilt, fear, and pain. She couldn't feel her heart. She sat on a metallic gray chair, closed her eyes, and tried to do what she was told to do: PRAY!

"Dear God!" She called in her heart, "Are you hearing me? I prayed for you five times a day but never felt connected. I know praying was just another duty in my daily schedule. I was told it's a must or else I would go to hell! I never talked to you; I don't know how I don't know if it is possible. Would you believe me if I prayed for you to bring back life to her? How could you believe me when for my whole life I said what I didn't mean? When I said I was ok when I wasn't? When I smiled while my heart was screaming out of my chest, crying, begging for help? How could you believe that she meant the world to me when I was too busy keeping up with my schedule that I only saw her on occasion? "And she opened her eyes so quickly in an attempt to run away from the one obvious truth: She indulged in the shallowness of life that she forgot who she was and what meant to her the most: her family! She was too busy taking and benefiting from each and every opportunity that came in her way that she forgot to give, to contribute, to care, and to love! She was too busy reaping the rewards as she was convinced that she had already paid her shares and the universe owed her everything she dreamed of that she skipped the life purpose: Contribution!

That night, she got a phone call from the family doctor who was collaborating with the other doctors in the hospital: "May her soul rest in peace; my deepest condolences to the whole family!". She used to hear and read these words but never knew what they really meant! She roared like a lion that just got a poisonous arrow in its chest... she ran into her empty house... hit the walls.... Put her hand on her heart; the pain was so unbearable that she wanted to take it off her chest and put it miles away from her.

She reached the hospital and waited for the doctors' approval to go in and see her sister. While she was waiting, EMS brought in a man who had severe injuries due to a fatal accident and whose screams were the only thing that could break the muteness of the ED at 1 AM in the morning. She contemplated him and asked herself: "Whose pain is bigger? They made pain killers for the whole body; what about the heart? How do we silence its anguish?". "Selena! We got you the approval; you can go in," said one nurse who cut off Selena's thoughts about heart agony and the unfounded medicine for it. She went in silently and heard the noise of the medical equipment growing louder with every step to find her sister Merida sleeping peacefully on the IC bed. The room was cold, colorless, lifeless. Everything felt gray. Merida was intubated. The oxygen was still going into her lungs, making her chest go up and back down. She ran to one of the nurses and asked her to come as she thought her sister might be alive. The nurse calmed her down and replied back to her with a sad yet confident tone: "Dear, her heart had stopped beating, there is no pulse. It's just the ventilator". She got closer to her sister's body and looked at her big charming closed eyes. "Oh my God! How beautiful you are!" She said to her in a gentle voice as if she did not want to wake her up. She put her fingers in her sister's soft hair, held her left hand, and laid her head delicately on her sister's front. Her hand was warm, as if she didn't leave yet. Although she didn't react, Selena felt that she was watching, hearing, and feeling her. Crying silently, she whispered to her, "Forgive me, sister. Maybe if I had held your hand from day 1, you could have fought to stay. Forgive me, sister; if I only knew you were leaving so early, I would have spent more time with you. Forgive me, sister; I was blind, and it is so painful to finally see. Forgive me, sister! I was dead, and I had just come back from my eternal coma. I loved you so much. I didn't know you meant the world to me until you left my world. Forgive me for judging you, for not allowing you to be, for not accepting the fact that you were different. I thought I was protecting you. Forgive my ignorance, sister. This is how I learned to love!". Then she got up, went to the end of the bed, held her sister's feet, and kissed them. She went back, laid her head on her sister's front, played "Ya-Sin", a Quranic verse Audio on her phone and started reading it to her.

"Indeed, it is We who bring the dead to life and record what they have put forth and what they left behind, and all things We have enumerated in a clear register", Selena was contemplating in silence these Sacred Quranic Words as if it was her first time reading them; the words hit her so hard that she was looking at Merida's immovable body and asking her sister "Merida, I know your soul is still here; your body is disconnected, but your soul will never be. Merida, you are reborn today, enjoy your new journey, sister, and I hope the other sacred world will be colorful heaven to you and as beautiful as your free soul. I love you, sister! "

It was then when her mother opened the door, stepped into the room, and kissed her beautiful Merida, a goodbye Kiss on her hands, her feet, and her front. She slept next to her daughter, held her hand, played with her beautiful hair, and mourned her quietly. "My little, my queen, my beautiful baby. Rest my butterfly. Rest in peace and love. Today, a piece of my heart has traveled with you to eternal heaven. I miss you already, but I know God will have mercy on you more than me. May God bless you, my daughter. I love you," and she read her Quraan in a soft yet heartbroken tone.

"Mama, it is so painful; I feel the emptiness of the whole universe in my chest. The oxygen is here, but I can not take it. Mama, would it get better with time? Would it go away?" reclaimed Selena, looking for a relieving answer.

"God will guide you through and show you the way out, my little. You are not alone, baby. God is always with you, and I will be always holding your hand." Replied her mom, assuring her that her pain would not last forever.

The funeral was everything but the usual funeral to be held in small villages like Baalbeck.

It was surprisingly quiet and peaceful. The only thing one can hear is the Quraan reading. The family decided not to go with the dramatic ordinary rituals. They asked the attendees to pay condolences silently as Merida's soul needs to leave peacefully. Selena was meditating just by looking at her sister. Question after question was popping up in her mind: "that's it? In a second, will one leave everything and go? What really matters? If this is not lasting, what is lasting? Are all the struggles that we go through in life worth it? Who am I? What am I doing here? Why was I born in the first place? Was I sent by coincidence? Why am I racing all the time? For what? With whom am I racing? With my own self?". Selena felt naked; for the first time in her life, she couldn't hide behind her family's name, her position, her appearance, nothing. It was only her!

She ran to the first floor, went into her room, locked the door, looked at her brownie eyes in the mirror, deeply focused on her dilating pupils, and surprisingly asked herself: "Who are you?" But the more she focused, the more she felt lost!

"What did you do with the time that was given to you?" She continued, shocked but eager to know. What did you add to the world? Did you really think you are here by coincidence? Are you really happy? When was the last time you genuinely laughed? When was the last time you were alive? Where is your soul? Who are you? Answer me!!! She shouted, afraid and uncertain!"

She went back to the funeral, sat in front of Merida, looked at her closed eyes, and realized that her sister was aware of the disconnection between Selena and Selena's own soul. Suddenly, all the nonsense of Merida became logical and understandable. She was right! Selena laughed when she should have cried, pretended to be proud of her truth, took where she should have given, and chosen war where she should have chosen peace. Selena's God was fear when she thought she worshiped Allah. She looked into her heart and realized that her God resembled what was in her heart. She never talked to God because he would have punished her and blamed her. She couldn't acknowledge his mercy since she was never merciful with herself. She lost her soul in the name of right and wrong, "we were raised this way," and logic. Thousands of "whys" were hitting her simultaneously, as if her whole life was meaningless and purposeless.

"Sister, I promise you I will never let my soul down anymore. I love you. Forgive me, and May God Forgive and Bless You. Thank you, Merida, for always being here for me". These were the last words Selena whispered to Merida before saying the last Goodbye.

And this is how Selena's journey of love and contribution started. She quit her job, left her country, changed her career path, and opened up for self-forgiveness, peace, and love. She now believes in inspiration; she now asks the right questions every morning. She now talks to GOD through love and compassion. She talks to GOD openly; she is no more afraid; she is powered by the Almighty "ALLAH". She realized that GOD wants her to grow and that she was sent because she had a message, and her message is unique and important. She knows that she is not her mind, nor her body, nor her emotions, nor her possessions, nor her name. She is none of that; she realizes that these are only the tools for her soul to flourish into her completeness. She is love; she is God's caliph, "Khalifa" or "successor" on earth!

So, what is death? Death is the transformation of earthly energy into an eternal one. It is the end of the earthly game and the beginning of eternal reality. As for the players who are still in the game, death is a wake-up call; it is GOD's way to guide our lost souls for them to transit from darkness to light and from fear to love. God is Love, God is peace, God is light. Whenever we realize this truth, we will realize that our dear ones pass away to continue elsewhere. We realize that GOD is much more merciful to make us suffer. It is we who tag death as unacceptable, traumatic, and unfair. It is we who choose to believe that death is separation. It is we who choose to believe that we can not connect to the unseen; therefore, we cannot connect to our loved ones. This is not God; this is the fear inside us that chose black to color death.

What color would I choose for death? I see death in Purple when I remember her smile. I see death in Red when I remember her courage and energy; I see death in pink when I feel her soft voice in my ears. I see death in hazel when I close my eyes and look deep into hers. I see death in black when I want to touch her hand, and I can't. I see death in white when I feel the clarity her death brought into my life. I see death in rainbow—I see death in colors!

This chapter is dedicated to My sister's soul Nada and her daughter Sandy without whom I would never go on this journey. I love you, Nada. And I adore you, Sandy.

ABOUT THE AUTHOR

SIBA YAGHI

SIBA YAGHI was born in Baalbeck, a city in Bekaa, Lebanon. She was raised in a conservative environment where women's freedom ended, and societal restrictions were imposed. She has a rebellious character and always looks for the "why" in every collective belief. Her mission is to help people understand why they do what they do so they can make better decisions and question cultural conformity.

After getting her bachelor's in Business Administration and Management, she started her career as a banker in Lebanon at the age of 21 and had the opportunity to work for many multinational and local corporations. To further expand her career options, she decided to pursue a Master's Degree in Banking and Finance.

After the death of her sister in 2020, she decided to move to Dubai to start over as a business development director in the Media and Marketing field, she has become a business coach and puts this down to her passion to understand people's and businesses' needs and desires.

For the past eight years, she has developed the *4W's Methodology* for decision-making based on her research of people's choices, processes, and motives and how they are interlinked with their beliefs. She is looking forward to sharing these on podcasts and virtual stages.

Connect with Siba here:

Email: siba.yaghi@hotmail.com

Instagram: https://www.instagram.com/siba_yaghi/

LinkedIn: https://www.linkedin.com/in/siba-yaghi/

YouTube: www.youtube.com/sibayaghi

JANE G. GOLDBERG, PhD

THE ILLUMINATIVE TRANSFORMATIVE POWER OF SCARIFICATION

*N*one of us escapes trauma. It is a consequence of living a human life. And with trauma comes the accompanying and inevitable scarring. Scars may manifest outwardly or inwardly, seen or invisible: with representation on the levels of physical or emotional, literal or metaphorical, profound or inconsequential. They may be deliberate or accidental.

Scars are both proof and reminders of our personal journeys, the paths we have taken, and the struggles we have endured. And they tell us, ultimately, of our own survival. They elaborate segments of our history–embodied within our bodies. I call them: museums of ourselves, our body/psyche/soul selves. They point us to our past, a needle on a treasure map directing our way back to the origin of the trauma, at times even back to an event that may have been buried too deeply, too painfully, for conscious remembrance. And, too, they point us toward our future, asking us to ponder the lesson and meaning the scar may hold for us.

Scars are the indicator of a breach, an injury, or a penetration. They tell tales of aggression, pain, and loss; but they also tell tales of acceptance, survival, attachment, and rebirth. When traumatic memories are activated, the scar, and the underlying wound, can be seen, processed, understood, and used as an endurable mark of illuminative transformation.

Although a scar is a mark of violation, it represents, as well, a natural healing response. The etymology of the word is instructive about the deepest connotation of scarring. The original Greek meaning is "hearth" or "fireplace." Scars are our home. We live in and with, and ultimately, beyond our scars. We need to find a home in our scars, embrace them, and find within them both safety and value.

Bodily scars arise from being wounded from an accident, a burn, surgery, acne, infection, or illness. Although scars present themselves externally on the skin, they are also present internally in organs and other tissues. The injury sets into motion a series of biochemical processes: normal tissues break; specialized fibroblasts cells are called into action; new connective tissue made up of collagen is produced. Scar tissue is different from the normal tissue that it has replaced. Instead of the random basketweave formation of the collagen fibers in unwounded skin, in scar tissue, the collagen creates an alignment formation in which all fibers follow a single direction. This difference affects the quality of the tissue, making it generally weaker, less resistant to ultraviolet radiation, and no longer able to support the growth of sweat and hair follicles. And while these biological processes describe physical scarring, they find symbolic representation in emotional scarring as well. Psychic scars, too, leave a residue of immobility and vulnerability. But, unlike physical scars, psychic scars led us to ongoing, continuous possibilities for emotional movement, mental flexibility, and psychological growth.

Emotional Scarring and a Sea of Red Ribbons

Emotional scarring arises from trauma that is the end result of events or experiences that leave the imprint of a deeply felt sense of unsafety and often helplessness. It can result from either one single event or can be part of ongoing experiences of abuse. Although the injury is initially emotional, the representation of the trauma is often stored in the bodies' tissues and can lead to physical manifestation as well.

As a psychoanalyst, I have been most interested in psychic scars. These are the ones we carry invisibly inside us. I believe that emotional scars constitute the most plentiful scars. I once ran a workshop on trauma and asked everyone to take a red cloth ribbon and pin it where they had scars, either physical or emotional. I chose red as the symbol of the blood that scarring stops from flowing interminably, thus serving a life preservative function. The room soon became a sea of red. Ribbons near the heart were the most plentiful.

I was not unlike my workshop's participants. I, too, wore a red ribbon. I placed it around my neck, where I have had a noticeable scar since I was 20. It is from when I had a razor blade slice open my neck while being raped, left for dead by a stranger who had broken into my apartment. This brutal event that created my scar was life-changing. It pained me; it pained my mother; it pained my boyfriend. And it took me off the course of the life plans that had been my vision all through college. Even more than the pain, my emotional scarring manifested as deep, unrelenting fear. Fear defined my life for a decade after. But I know that the event, and the subsequent suffering I endured, gave me a depth of understanding of psychic pain, sensitivity to emotional suffering, and an empathic acceptance of mental distress. I know that I wouldn't be the psychoanalyst, friend to others, and mother to my daughter that I am today without having had that experience.

My Mother, Tina Fey, the Look, and Gender Connections

For much of my life, I saw my mother's scar where her breast had once been. I remember the day she showed me. I was terrified to look. I understood that it was going to be an unpretty sight. Yet, she insisted I look. She wanted me to feel comfortable seeing it. I saw much more than her scar. I saw the visible evidence of a strong, even courageous woman, dissolving walls while boldly proclaiming who she now was, announcing the new her —the one who she had become.

A 1993 *New York Times Magazine* cover featured a photograph of a breast cancer survivor. As my mother had forced me to look, Joanne Motichka similarly forced the world to look at this shocking self-portrait photograph of a woman with a deep scar instead of where her breast belonged. Mail from readers arrived at the magazine as a deluge, and it became and remained one of the most controversial images in the magazine's history.

Non-breasted women have led the way in the path of redefining womanhood. We know, from these women, as well as from understanding the historical roots of scarification, that one of the primary issues with scarring is precisely about identity. Who am I? How do I look? How do I look to myself and to the world? What is the connection between how I look and how I feel about myself? What is the connection to how I look and who I am, who I was, and who I want to be?

While women with breast scars are generally rated as less attractive, minor facial scars on women can be an asset. Writer, actor, and comedian Tina Fey was five years old when a stranger slashed her face. The remnant of that experience is her still-visually prominent scar. As she describes in her autobiography, she feels that her scar has invited kindness and a protective concern from strangers.

Severe scars that disfigure the face, however, are seen as not only unattractive—but, at times—a sign of bad character. One study found that people with facial disfigurement are seen as being emotionally unstable, untrustworthy, unhappy, and less intelligent. Gender also looms large in people's feelings about scars. One study found that women rated men with facial scars as desirable for short-term relationships, but they showed an equal preference for scarred and unscarred men for long-term relationships.

The Historical Roots of Scarification

For most of human history, scars were deliberately crafted. In spite of the process being exceedingly painful, it was performed in many cultures all over the planet. Rock paintings from 6000 B.C. in Algeria show people decorated with dots and lines. The remains of the Iceman, estimated to be 5200 years old, similarly shows evidence of purposeful scarification. African scarification is traced back to 4000 BC, and ancient Egyptian writings date the practice to 1700 BCE. References to scarification have also been found in Polynesia, Peru, Greenland, Japan, China, Chile, Italy, Austria, and Alaska.

In the past, any part of the body could become a canvas for the creation of indelible markings. The process was accomplished through cutting with a scalpel or a cauterizing tool in order to create grooves in the skin. The most painful technique, called strike branding, is essentially the same process used today for cattle branding. After the scars had been created, soot was rubbed into the open wounds, serving as both a darkening color as well as an additional irritant. The flesh would then be pressed against, forcing an increase in the swelling with the effect of raising the welts above the level of the surface of the skin. Often a hook (sometimes a tool as primitive as a fishhook) was used to simulate the raised skin further to become even more prominent and pronounced.

We must ask: why would individuals, even whole tribes embrace a custom that is a deliberate maiming, a calculated affliction of pain, as well as a potentially dangerous, even life-threatening act.

Our ancient ancestors highly valued their scars. Men who exhibited raised welts were viewed as brave and looked fierce in battle. As they were considered to be the most fearless men in the tribe, their tattooed wheels made them especially attractive to women.

But ancestral scarring meant much more than beauty and recognition of courage; it meant identity. African tribes used the scars for the purpose of classification of its members: age, life experience, sexual maturity, members of families, and members of the tribes. We can think of scars as ancestral identity cards. In ancient Greece, men were identified by their scars for the signing of legal documents. If there was no scar, the man was labeled *dsemos*: "not marked." The absence of scarring meant the absence of actual personhood. Both Greeks and Romans used scarring to identify individuals as belonging to a specific group of people: nobility, criminals, or members of a specific religious order were all marked differently and distinctively. The Maori men in New Zealand had etched scars covering their entire faces until the late 1800s. As with our more ancient ancestors, these etchings were each unique and indicated individuality.

Still today, some African tribes retain the tradition of scarification, serving, as it did long ago, as a rite of passage. In Sudan and Ethiopia, the procedure initiates boys into manhood, entering them into their new adult position in society. The *gaar* ceremony involves cutting six parallel lines across their foreheads, thus preparing them to marry, own cattle, and fight battles. Sudanese girls, too, receive marks as they mature from puberty, menstruation, and again after weaning their first child.

The physical sensations from both the procedure as well as the aftermath were an important part of the process. How the pain was endured from the administration of the scarring procedure was seen as significant by the tribe members. Young men exhibited the quality of discipline by enduring the pain without complaint. Even today, pain tolerance is valued. Paul Bohannan, an anthropologist who visited the Tiv tribe in Nigeria, asked about the pain and was told: "Of course it is painful. What girl would look at a man if his scars had not cost him pain?" Anthropologist Victoria Ebin maintains that still today, scars are also considered to enhance a woman's sexual appeal and that raised scars induce strong erotic feelings when touched.

Scarification, Monsters of the Mind, and Fairy Tales

Psychoanalyst and author Bruno Bettelheim understood exposure to fairy tales in childhood encourages emotional maturity. The actual contents of fairy tales are distressing and reflect both physical danger and deep emotional discomfort. Rather than the children in the stories feeling and being safe, they typically have lost a parent; they are often kidnapped, made horribly unhappy, and even tortured. They are scared. The protagonists in these tales must engage in Herculean struggles to resolve their predicaments. Their successes in meeting the challenges, in facing suffering with courage and determination, and their ability to emerge victoriously, transforms them into the heroes and heroines from whom we can learn. Bettelheim suggests that these ancient tales are not mere fluff childhood stories; rather, they are lessons and inductions into psychological growth that reflect an essential aspect of life and life's ongoing difficulties. Bettelheim emphasized that fairy tales serve the function of preparing children for the exigencies of later life.

I believe that deliberate scarification serves the same function as fairy tales. Both are part of a hardening process that prepares the recipient for life's physical and emotional trials. Although the painful rituals of scarification are themselves traumatic, the ordeal is viewed as a welcome test of toughness. The scars reflect the rewards, the sign that one has become a new person worth admiration and respect.

The Scar Each and Every One of Us Shares: Humans and Some Plants Too

With or without deliberate scarification, each of us retains visible evidence of our individual personhood: our belly button is the remnant of the cutting of the umbilical cord, the final and irreversible event of separation from the life-giving source of our mothers' bodies. Freud identified the birth trauma as the most significant trauma that each of us faces. I don't think Freud was speaking hyperbolically. He felt that we spend the rest of our lives recovering from the trauma of separation from the breach of the original biological symbiosis with mother. Yet, because of the birth trauma, we become transformed into independent selves: glorious self-governing, self-regulating, self-determining selves.

Humans develop larger scars than any other animal. One theory to explain the magnification of human scarring suggests that scarring developed alongside human intelligence. As we started relying on our brains instead of our instincts to help us escape from dangerous situations, scars served the purpose of reminding us of our past mistakes.

It is interesting to note that deliberate scarification exists as a practice in botany for plants as well as for humans. Seeds of many plant species are impervious or resistant to water and gases; but water and gases are important biological components to facilitate the germination of the seed. A farmer can decide to open or modify the coat of a seed (analogous to the skin of a human) through mechanical, thermal, or chemical intervention. This process, also called scarification, speeds up the natural processes of the seed coat, opening itself to the water and gasses necessary for growth. As plants thrive through scarification, we find that humans, too, grow through the healing of scars.

The New Scarring

Today, deliberate skin etching has had a resurgence. Rather than the carved markings protruding out from the skin, contemporary markings are vividly colored. Of course, this form of color scarification is called "tattoos." In the U.S. and other Western countries, tattooing has become an ever-growing practice, as larger and larger numbers of people are choosing to express their identities by colorful body markings. One poll revealed that 36 percent of 25- to 29-year-olds in the U.S. have one or more tattoos. As well, contemporary tattooing has acquired a different social meaning: unlike raised scarification, which has deep meaning in terms of group membership, today's tattoos are more reflective of individual desires and experiences.

When we become interested in the personal significance of our scars, we can begin to see the relationship between our unconscious, our wounds, and our history. Every emotional wound is a historical scar. Scars, either physical or psychological, tell us much about who we are; but they are also reminders of who we were, as well as who we became from an experience/event that cannot and should not be forgotten. They are like a bodily diorama, depicting the traumas and challenges of our past, our identity of who we are, and our dreams of who we can become. Our past, present, and future meet in the scarred representation on our bodies.

Perhaps, though, the deepest meaning is scarification is spiritual. Our ancestors believed that when a symbol was tattooed onto a member of the tribe, a spiritual power was lent to him or her. The process and the subsequent scarred display provided a cleansing of the soul. Among the most popular motifs of primitive tribes was the frigate bird, which is connected to the Birdman deity. This god represents "the host of the spirit of the dead." The process of scarification connects us not only to ourselves but to all of mankind, both those deceased and those still alive.

To be human is to be scarred. As we, our children, our parents, and virtually everyone alive, develop scars around the world crisis we find ourselves in today, it may be useful to think about trauma as a process of endlessly becoming and of ongoing re-defining of ourselves. The physical, psychological, sacred, spiritual, and mystical elements of tattoos confer healing, memories, revelation, awareness, integration, and the power of wholeness. Ultimately, most deeply, they are stories of the soul.

ABOUT THE AUTHOR

JANE G. GOLDBERG, PhD

JANE G. GOLDBERG, Ph.D., is an oncological psychoanalyst, a psychologist, and the author of eight books, including the critically acclaimed, *The Dark Side of Love,* and her two most recent books, *My Mother, My Daughter, My Self,* and *The Hormesis Effect.* Dr. Goldberg is a prolific blogger with her newsletter MusingsFrom20thStreet.com. She is the owner of two wellness centers: Dr. Jane's La Casa in NYC, celebrating its 30th year anniversary, and La Casa Spa & Wellness Puerto Rico, a destination center in the Puerto Rican rain forest, celebrating its 38th year of operation.

In integrating her dual passions for holistic health and psychoanalysis, Dr. Goldberg's therapeutic approach is truly and deeply mind/body healing. She is, as well, the Founder and Director of Brainercize, a system of interactive brain exercise classes designed to maximize brain functioning (brainercize.org). Her next book project is companion pieces: The Revolutionary Mind Project and The Evolutionary Brain Project, which are all planned for publication in 2023.

Connect with Jane here:

Website: https://drjanegoldberg.com

Special offers: free infrared sauna at my center in NY, free infrared sauna at the center in NY, (www.LaCasaSpa.com) with another therapy booking, or a free stay with a 3-day booking in Puerto Rico.

(http://LaCasaSpaAndWellnessPuertoRico.com)

PART II

FOLLOWING THE FLOW

KEEN BEING

FLOWING INTO THE DARKNESS: NO STORY BOOK BEGINNING

"I don't feel that it is necessary to know exactly what I am. The main interest in life and work is to become someone else that you were not in the beginning. If you knew when you began a book what you would say at the end, do you think that you would have the courage to write it?

What is true for writing and for a love relationship is true also for life. The game is worthwhile insofar as we don't know what will be the end". - Michael Foucault

This story doesn't begin with "once upon a time", nor end in... "and they lived happily ever after". This story is the real story of how I turned my shadow into my greatest ally.

Even as I write this, I'm not sure exactly what will come forward. If I scripted everything out, I would lose the flow and the inherent wisdom that lives beyond me within the story itself. My ego would diligently edit out the rawness and the reality of some of the things I've experienced in life that I would otherwise not have the courage to share. I would be caught in the perpetual self-reinforcing loop that we all play in - attempting to project an idealized image of myself for you, dear reader. The one that I thought I wanted everyone to see.

This is a different sort of story. I've found part of life's challenge, opportunity, and purpose is to fully awaken to the authenticity of who we are. And, once we do, we get access to an incredible gift. We get to leave behind the unconscious patterning, wounding, and trauma that has become so much a part of the human experience.

My sincerest wish in offering this story to you is that it may create a window through which you might climb. A window into a world where you all are invited to peer closely within and fully embrace all of yourself - the good, the bad, and the ugly. A world where you may come to trust that by welcoming, exploring, loving, and receiving all of the wisdom and intelligence that lies within every single part of you, you will receive the greatest gift of all. You will receive your capacity to skillfully choose beyond the limiting patterns and hamster wheels you have been spinning within and regain your agency in creating the more loving world your soul knows is possible.

What I've learned is that EVERY part of our life matters. Every curve and turn we take, every pothole we hit, every face-plant, every peak and valley - they can all become powerful tools in unfurling the fullest expression of ourselves. Suppose we're fully willing to receive the teachings available in them... what possibilities for real change await?

In order to do this, we must be willing to look through this window of truth and allow life's most bitter lessons to become a catalyst for our unique transformation. Our ability to be with our darkest secrets is directly correlated with the opportunity for our truest liberation.

Through the path of deep awareness and presence, we have an opportunity to alchemize the seemingly destructive parts of ourselves consciously. Only from that vantage point can we begin to move into our higher expressions of integrity, clarity, and purpose for our own personal well-being and enjoyment, as well as for the betterment of humanity.

Shadow As Ally

In life, there are critical choice points and opportunities that come along which provide us with the perfect set of circumstances to produce radical shifts. Little did I know that a decision I made nearly 20 years ago would impact my life in such a pivotal way, forever altering its course.

To tell this story properly, I must first provide some context. I was raised very conservatively as a Jehovah Witness. I was not allowed to have friends outside of the church, no celebration of holidays, no rated "R" movies, no TV during the week, no Saturday morning cartoons, no girlfriends, no relationship with women outside of friendship, and no masturbation. Beyond that, higher university education was discouraged, and we were expected to devote our lives to study and ministry. From an early age, I was expected to go to church three times a week and on average, spend 20 hours a month knocking on our neighbors' doors, spreading the "gospel."

So there I was, at the Airport in Vegas, waiting for a return flight home from a business trip. On the heels of my 30th birthday where the shadowy seeds of my shameless desire would take root. Simultaneously, it birthed within me a transcendental state of altered consciousness and a deep mystical awareness that I had never experienced before.

For the previous three years, I had already begun the process of metamorphosis into someone entirely new. Having been raised with such strict standards, the reality of my home life and having been married at an early age fused with my newly formed love for philosophy and personal development (as a result of going back to school to finish my university degree) - Vegas, that summer, was probably the worst thing for me to experience. Inside the lights, glitz, glamour, smell of cigarettes, alcohol, and sex... I felt a distinct call to freedom.

Like many other married people who venture away to Vegas alone, I felt pulled to explore the outward edges of my repressed desires. I soon learned where the catchphrases about Las Vegas, such as 'Sin City' and 'What happens in Vegas stays in Vegas', earned their origin. I was counting on it.

So there I was, lying in bed, unable to sleep. With the constant pulse of raging nightlife outside of my window throbbing in my ears, I could feel a pounding and pulling within me to explore the debauchery of my surroundings, a call to explore the forbidden fruit of my upbringing in the church.

As I continued to allow my imagination to wander, before I knew it, I was hypnotically drawn from my bed and found myself thinking - "I'm going to see for myself!". I realized that if I was going to answer the nagging questions in my head about whether the world was as vile as I had been told,

I needed to know if it was founded in truth. I needed to find my answers in real-time and in the FLESH.

The smartest phone I had then was a work-issued blackberry whose internet connection was practically nil. Instead of relying upon the ease and convenience of a personal handheld device, I had to do this the old-fashioned way. I found the 24-hour business center of my hotel, got online, and began my search. The thrill and intensity of the very act of even typing "Best strip clubs in Vegas" into the browser and anticipating (yes, search engines were much slower then) the results felt like being given a shot of pure adrenaline. Before I knew it, I was outside hailing a taxi and on my way to dance with my shadow. And fall in love (with a stripper).

Leilani danced effortlessly, moved with a sensuality that was fully consumed in the being of her own erotic bliss. Our eyes locked, and suddenly, without any warning - a tantric poet was in the process of being born. After her set, she sat next to me - I was sweating and, at the same time, mesmerized by her grace.

The conversation flowed just as effortlessly as the way she moved and touched something my heart had been aching to receive. Even if what she offered was all just a performance, what resulted was me doing the unthinkable and going back the next day to ask her out. To my great surprise, she said yes. My shadow was driving, but I was inflow.

We met down on the Vegas Strip, and I accompanied her to pick up a gift she purchased for a cousin, and then we went off to dinner. We laughed, told stories, and closed down the restaurant. At the end of dinner, as we were walking through the Aladdin, we came across a gallery and were both caught by a painting in the window called, *The Red Purse by Vladmir Kush.*

I didn't realize it at the time, but this experience created the perfect storm form for my shadow to come out and play. Had I only known how significant this moment would prove to be. Stumbling across this artwork under this particular set of circumstances would help me open up to my inner artist and steer the direction of my life. Years later, this connection to art reawakened in me an undiscovered gift for writing ekphrastic poetry. Fast forward nearly ten years later, I found myself in an entirely new profession as an Art Consultant in a gallery, selling fine art and pairing it with my poetry. In fact, as fate would have it, the gallery where I landed my first art job carried the work of the very same artist. When I walked into that gallery for my interview, positioned right in the middle of the foyer was a bronze sculpture based upon the same exact painting. "Shadow as Ally," I thought to myself as I laughed.

As Leilani and I stared at the art, we both began to comment on our interpretation of the painting. If you have never seen this powerful piece, it is a surrealist portrayal of a red clutch purse. The two sides of the clasp that close the purse are the head of a woman on one side and the head of a man on the other. They seemed to be locked in a kiss but they couldn't fully embrace because the purse was so full of money that it could not be closed.

While there were many ways to interpret this, as I reflected on the painting, I realized that it evoked a feeling of what was happening inside my marriage. My wife and I had differing opinions regarding material gain, the acquisition of money, and how it was to be used, and it was starting to create a major disconnection in our relationship.

I contrasted this with my experience with Leilani. Although her selected profession was rooted in what is often characterized as a seedy and unsafe environment in which abuse and exploitation are rampant, she insisted on paying for half the dinner and provided many hints throughout the evening that she wasn't looking for money in our connection.

As we got back to our cars, we embraced, and she tried to kiss me. Being a married man and a Jehovah Witness at the time, where in fact I was considered an elder to be looked up to, my conscience was screaming at me…"NO, NO, NO"! As she leaned in, I awkwardly turned my face, not allowing her lips to touch mine.

I got in my rental car, and as I drove away, my mind was bombarded with so many feelings and thoughts. One was exhilaration, "Whoa, I dodged a bullet, but that was amazing!". The other, anxiety and guilt thinking - "What have I done, I am such a sinner".

The next day waiting for my flight to leave Vegas, I found my initial dread began to dissipate as I drifted off in a daydream of my encounter with Leilani. This was my first brush with the experience of an altered state of consciousness. I experienced a temporary state of sublime bliss and was anchored deeply in the present moment. As I looked out through the floor-to-ceiling large 30-foot glass windows of the tarmac, the fog lifted miraculously, and the sky cleared instantaneously. The most beautiful poetry began to automatically pour out of my pen and into my journal. My shadow side had birthed the poet within.

Curiosity Saved the Cat!

When I got home, the guilt returned and began to riddle me from within. Already feeling the friction of discord in my marriage and now laden with shame, subconsciously, I began to pull away. I was consumed with guilt and well on my way into the descent of my darkness.

My connection with Leilani left my shadow thirsting for more. Fast forward four months later, I came home early from a trip with my wife without her. Feeling the tension of our crumbling marriage, I sought relief and pleasure from the pressure I was feeling.

Now, before I share what transpired, you have to really imagine how green I was. At the time, I had no first-hand knowledge of what happens out in the "real" world. I grew up as the proverbial "golden child," who excelled at being the first in everything spiritual. At 18, I was appointed as the equivalent of a deacon, and then fast forward ten years later, appointed as an elder in the church - either of which very rarely ever happened. The average minimum age of most deacons was appointed at the age of 25, and elders at the age of 35. In the Jehovah's Witness church, I was somewhat of a prodigy. I was married at 21 and lost my virginity on my wedding night...yes, I was that guy.

With my wife nearly 3,000 miles away, I was again free and curious. Taking to the internet, I searched Craigslist for "sensual massage". My only context for what was involved in this type of massage was from co-workers on the construction site I worked in my early twenties. I didn't know what a "happy ending" was and figured I would just go in, get the message, and forgo the ending part.

I called the establishment, booked a time, and showed up a few hours later. To my surprise, the location I arrived at was an apartment building. Odd, I thought but proceeded anyway. I knocked on the door and was greeted by a kind and gracious young Asian woman. She proceeded to escort me to the bedroom, told me to take a shower, and then go to the massage table.

As the massage progressed, I recall thinking to myself..."Wow, this is really intimate, is this supposed to be part of the package?". She climbed on top of the massage table and before I even realized what was happening, she slipped on a condom and went way past the point of a "happy ending".

When I got home, I broke out my bible, crying, reading scripture after scripture, mortified at what I had just done. A few days later, when my wife returned, I tried to pretend nothing had happened. My conscience and puritan beliefs began to eat me alive. "How could I do this?" I thought. As the guilt festered like an undressed wound, I couldn't take the fiery heat of my own misstep and began to blame my wife.

Riddled with trauma from seeing her father cheat on her mother as a child, she had a fear embedded within her that I would also cheat, accusing me of being too flirty with the women in the church. Similar to the story of Adam and Eve, my ego said to myself..."She made me do this; if only she treated me better - none of this would have happened."

With this level of self-deception, my spirit continued to be hardened, and I pointed the finger with increasing intensity. This created even more tension, combined with my guilt and her voice nagging in my head, "You are going to cheat on me." I got to the point where I snapped inside, internalized it, and absolved myself of all responsibility at the same time. "Yes, I am a cheater because of you, and I will find a different woman to cheat with for every year we have been married," became my new mantra.

Over the course of three years, I allowed my spirit to turn bitter, and I now sought the darkness, making it a regular habit to visit the shadowy underbelly world of strip clubs. While I did end up connecting with other women, I didn't follow through with my original intent to have sex with a different woman every year of my marriage.

However, my decision to surrender to the darkness led me down such a treacherous descent that I could no longer live with myself and had to come clean. The guilt was literally eating me alive to the point where "coming clean" plummeted me into a deep but hidden depression. I was unwilling to squarely face what I had done. So, I toyed with a thought I never imagined I would - I contemplated suicide. After writing my "goodbye" letter to my family, I realized that taking myself out of the game of life wasn't an option

I had the courage to follow through with. What was required was even more courageous, though; I HAD to tell the truth.

On the evening of my last visit to the strip club, I called my Dad, who was working the graveyard shift, and told him that something terrible had happened and I needed to talk to him right away. He told me to come to his workplace so that we could talk. When I arrived, I broke down crying, confessing everything I had done over the previous three years. Having had a rocky start to adulthood with his own demons and the trauma he suffered as a result of his two tours in Vietnam, I wasn't prepared for his response. When I finished spilling my guts out, he said to my surprise..."Is that all you did?". He went on to reassure me that by confessing, I would be forgiven.

The next day I told my wife—who, needless to say—was devastated but initially supportive, thinking we could work on our marriage and move past it. Now came the part for me to meet with the elders in the congregation. Sitting there before a "judicial body" of three elders, I confessed my "sins," and instead of accepting responsibility, I was still in the self-righteous blame game - caught in the grand delusions of my own inability to truly take full ownership of what I had done. Trapped in the story of the archetype of the golden child, I thought to myself, "All of this has to be someone else's fault; I could never have done such things on my own device."

I stepped out of the meeting room as they deliberated for over an hour, anxiously waiting - worrying what my punishment would be. Having served as an elder and sitting on several judicial cases myself, I knew that whenever someone confessed, they were never actually excommunicated from the church. I thought my case wouldn't end otherwise. My shadow had a different agenda.

Back inside their chambers, the presiding elder opened his bible and read to me a scripture that, in hindsight, was actually true, "For in his own eyes he flatters himself too much to detect and hate his error" (Psalm 36:2). After finishing reading the passage, I heard the verdict..."It is because of your deception, not what you did, that we have unanimously decided to disfellowship you from the Christian congregation." And with that, my world fell apart. Within an instant, everyone I loved, my family, friends since childhood...everyone in my community would begin to shun me. From that point forward, they would cease having any association with me whatsoever, not even saying a greeting to me or sitting down to eat a meal with me. The word devastation does not do justice to describe the severity of this blow.

With the rendering of that judgment, my wife decided that she wanted a divorce, telling me that if I got reinstated into the church, we could remarry.

Now alone in the dark and feeling into the depths of despair of isolation from losing everyone I loved, I had no choice but to figure out who I was.

Out of the Darkness

After having gone through a long, arduous journey exploring my shadow, I've learned the truth of Socrates' iconically famous quote, "The unexamined life is not worth living." Because of my inherent love for humanity, I have come to understand the crucial importance of taking a hard look within. If we desire a deep transformation of ourselves, we must be willing to look under every nook and cranny. Beyond this, we need to have the courage then to surrender to the evolutionary process of awakening and choose to live a conscious life.

Now more than ever, this in-depth self-examination is crucial for the well-being of this planet and humanity as a whole. If we are unable to make an accurate assessment of ourselves and then make the necessary adjustments, how can we truly make a significant difference in the world and courageously implement the changes needed to address the crisis the world so desperately needs to in our day and age?

In 2007, I received a divinely gifted poem in a dream that was initially inspired by an encounter I had with a spirit inspired woman I had met at a strip club the year before, right around the time I was excommunicated. The distress of being alone and in a deep state of grief and despair created the conditions for a spontaneous mystical experience to appear within me, which would forever awaken me to a deep realization of unity consciousness and the inherent beauty found within the human soul.

Following that awakening, I continued to receive more poetry. I was pulled towards a greater vision, learning how to trust messages and synchronicities that would inevitably move me closer to my dreams. None of that would have been possible if I had not surrendered to my shadow and then conducted an honest and thorough investigation into the inner workings of my psyche. I have developed a deep desire to understand the gifts of the shadow and, and explored this through many avenues and tools - studying with ancient plant medicine teachers, retreats in total darkness, silence, and beyond. I have made it a part of my mission to help others embrace their shadow as a gateway to an evolved state of consciousness. Learning to fully embrace the shadow is key to expanding ourselves to merge with oneness and enter into the state of nonduality and pure being.

In my upcoming spiritual memoir, "Shadow As Ally - One Man's Journey to the Light Through Darkness'—which is anticipated for release in 2024—I'll share my entire story and encourage people to understand that:

No matter how difficult the journey, we all have an ally in our shadow who can help us find the brilliant light within.

All we need is a little skillful guidance and the willingness and courage to take an intimate look inward and see what lies on the other side of belief and possibility. I invite you to join me in exploring and giving yourself the precious gift of knowing yourself in a more intimate way.

If you feel called to unfold the deep gifts of your own shadow, I would be honored to connect. I hold people through a 12-week process where we deepen your understanding of your unique life story, deconstruct the patterns of your shadow, and mine your incredible gifts. This process is designed to help you fully align with life and joyously return your soul to its highest expression as a conscious creator for the betterment of humanity.

"Staying within the lines is difficult, and sometimes we stray to find out who we are. But, if you don't color your life within the boundaries of your values, you won't illuminate the masterpiece that mother nature intended." - Keen

ABOUT THE AUTHOR

KEEN BEING

KEEN BEING is co-founder of Sol-Evolve, a speaker, coach, energy healer, and certified yoga and meditation teacher, passionate about the actualization of human potential. Keen has dedicated decades to living, mapping, and supporting teams and leaders on their own growth and development path in both government and private business sectors.

As a visionary, alchemist, poet, and medicine man; he is committed to helping leaders and trailblazers harness their full power by weaving together modern science, art and ancient wisdom with best business practices.

Drawing upon various healing modalities, coaching practices and techniques, Keen masterfully dances between the subtleness of the unconscious mind and the deep wisdom of the soul to skillfully unearth the latent knowledge hidden inside human consciousness.

With more than 25 years of leadership and public speaking, Keen is available for keynote speaking, leading immersive three, six and twelve month coaching and/or retreat journey's designed to help individuals or organizations to confront the transformational challenges facing our world today.

Connect with Keen here:

Website: https://www.sol-evolve.com/workingwithkeen

Freebie: Guided Meditation and 30 min Shadow Analysis Coaching Call: https://www.sol-evolve.com/giftoffering/

For all socials and to book a call: https://linktr.ee/keen.being

KATHERINE ZORENSKY

REMEMBERING THE FEMININE MYSTERIES

THE INITIATION OF GIVING BIRTH

*M*y entrance into the feminine mysteries didn't come through a workshop, a book, or a mentor. The mystery 'found' me through the birth of my children. In other words, it was not something I had to go seeking. It was something that initiated me as I found the courage to open up my life as it was.

What are the feminine mysteries? To me, they are innate wiring that gives us a means of accessing and being "Love" through our bodies, our actions, and our words. In simple, our feminine embodiment gives us the capacity to choose love over fear in each moment, each crossroads of our lives. These choices influence the trajectory of our relationships, our service, and our awakening.

Don't get me wrong; I've spent thousands of hours visiting sacred sites and delving deeply into the practice and tantric sciences to open and activate my electromagnetic channels. I have even created my own teaching platform bringing these ancient mysteries to modern women. However, no practice or meditation can challenge and integrate our deep feminine essence into our hearts and minds more directly than life itself. If we cannot live all that we have cultivated into our most mundane and intimate experiences, it has little significance on the evolution of ourselves and humanity. As we embrace our experience in our bodies and our hearts, we are forged deeper into love and forge the path for human consciousness deeper into love.

A Journey into the Unknown

My first pregnancy and birth were a journey into the unknown. I took my cues from my connection with the natural world and my body. It was a journey in trusting my instincts and intuition and the deep scripted knowing of birth through my body as it had been done since the beginning of human time.

Early on in my pregnancy, my daughter suggested through dreams that she wanted to be born in the ocean. After finding a midwife on the Big Island of Hawaii who would support us in our attempt at an ocean birth, we moved there.

The Big Island is powerful, alive, and raw. It was exactly the energy for me to delve into in my third trimester to harness and dance in the powerful energies coming through the ocean, the fiery volcano, and the fertile land. I spent hours with my bare feet in the sand, spiraling my hips, just allowing life, the sheer force of primal Earth, to move in and through me.

For weeks, I scoured the western shoreline to find the exact place my daughter wanted to be born. I found a small tide pool protected from the big waves by massive black lava guardian rocks. The pool was cleansed with gentle rushes of fresh ocean water and warmed by the sun. It was on a remote peninsula removed from traffic, yet only 10 minutes from the hospital. The moment I stumbled upon it and sank my toes into the soft sandy bottom, my body gave me a resounding "YES!" This was the entry point for my daughter from the womb into the world.

For the next 40 days, I woke early to swim with the dolphins in this bay. I spent hours twirling, playing, silently swimming, and floating with them. A few in the pod took a special interest in me, sometimes coming up underneath me and rubbing belly to belly. The moment I submerged my head in the water and heard the dolphins, my daughter began to kick! She, too, was connecting with her friends.

These mornings were ecstatic for me; the rising slant of golden sun filtering through the turquoise waters and the joyful exchange with these loving and joyful beings filled my heart. Soft undulating waves held me suspended while I released any remaining fear of the unknown surrounding birth. The dolphins and the ocean were an ever-beckoning invitation for me to relax into the joy of pregnancy and birth.

One morning I began feeling rushes while I was a good way out from shore with the dolphins. I broke off from the pod and swam my way back into shore flanked by two guardian dolphins. They accompanied me until I safely reached the shallows. Once upon the land, I sat down to catch my breath and sink deeper into the rhythmic intensity building within me.

After I dried in the sun, my daughter's father came in from his swim and escorted me to a small clearing in the nearby jungle. We had come prepared (just in case) with plenty of water and food, and it was here that I labored all day long. With each oncoming rush, I would reach for the strong stringy vines of the trees and hang, spiraling my hips in wider and wider circles. I danced, totally losing myself in the energy of the island, the nearby waves, and the rushes coursing through me. I danced in between the veils and felt my feet grounded on the earth and my heart buoyant and blissful with hormones and blessings of birthing.

The rushes intensified as I watched the brilliant orange sun drop below the horizon. My energy dropped even deeper inward. All around me was a soft hue of purple light. We felt our way to the edge of the water near the tide pool and set up a thick pad on the lava rock.

I surrendered on all fours, rocking and moving. The intensity of energy within me was building, and it felt more than I could hold. As soon as I recognized the tiny torch of my Midwife approaching us, my pelvis relaxed. She wordlessly put her hand on my low back and helped the energy move through.

II opened to the support of her hands and of my partner's body. The vortex of energy from above and below began to intensify, and suddenly my companions' support wasn't enough. I needed to be held by something far vaster. I felt like a caged animal. I could hear and feel their thoughts, doubts, fears, and anticipations.

I told them it was time for me to get into the water. They both supported me over the jagged rocks into the pool. I sat down on the soft sand and felt the cool water gather around me, like a welcoming hug, relaxing my whole body.

The moon shone its silvery light down into the pool, bringing a surreal luminescence.

The ocean waves reached high for the moon and crashed down in a spectacular display just beyond the guardian lava rocks of my protected tide pool. My womb resounded dancing, reaching, expanding, and contracting. The matched intensity inside and out enabled a relaxation in my body and mind. I dissolved in the vastness between waters and womb, and before I knew it, my daughter emerged into my midwife's hands amidst tiny fish in the soft, sandy tide pool.

The power of my first birth experience blew me wide open. I fully surrendered to my inner guidance and the guidance of the natural world. This strengthened my trust and empowered me. I found the true Womb Shaman within. I experienced the interconnection and one-ness that I had only conceptually understood before. In the birthing moments, I was held by the mother ocean and could open my yoni, womb, and heart to a further expanse of my soul.

However, this was not sustainable for me beyond those moments. There was no human structure in place for my 'return.' My life outside the birthing tide pool did not support me. As soon as I left these safe and sacred waters and walked on the rocky land, I felt the jagged sharpness of the lava rock underneath my feet and the harsh reality of a loveless relationship and no community to welcome me home.

I had done everything possible to ensure that my daughter would be born in the right place, but I had done nothing to set up the network I needed to return home from experience into daily human life. Though I was connected to my body, intuition, and nature, I had no real connection to the community, no real love for my daughter's father, and no means to communicate the experience to anyone.

Something so beautiful became registered in my psyche and body as trauma because the initiation was not completed. I was in denial of my vulnerable human needs.

The three years following were depressive and painful. I went on, and off medication, and the relationship ended after a grueling court battle. The cost of this access to 'oneness' through my womb was painful and isolating. My circuitry and remembrance were opening, but I was missing some major pieces of how to integrate this transcendent knowing into my human experience.

This birth only became a rite of passage for me when I found the support to do the necessary healing and re-integration. When I became pregnant with my next child, I was open and available to have a more supported and connected birth experience.

It was a Tuesday evening when rushes started. I went into the bedroom to dance and move to the music. My son's Papa began weaving a cocoon, with music, prayer, movement, chants, incense, and fire, adjusting and readying the physical and spiritual environments, creating a field of safety, love, and high-frequency sound.

Another rush came on. I moved with the intensity and spilled my laughter as joy, spiraling my hips downward and feeling a simultaneous spiral moving up through my heart and through my crown.

The midwives were called, and when they arrived, the rushes were in full swing! They checked my son's heartbeat and my dilation. Suddenly something felt stuck and not progressing; I felt a bubble of fear rise up and saw two roads in front of me. One led toward fear, hospitalization, and giving up my power. The other led to trust, surrender, strength, and perseverance. I felt and released this fear by talking to Papa for guidance, who received me and confirmed me. I made some physical adjustments to my cervix and hips, and with the next rush opened to surrender.

The pain dissolved into intensity, and I engaged in the dance again. I met the sensation full on with all of my body and all of my soul, welcoming it, welcoming him, feeling pushed to open beyond what I felt I could. There was a short reprieve, then the next rush came, asking me to surrender deeper and yet stay strong with my presence. I was a cat both rolling onto my back, softening to a belly rub, and roaring like a lion to meet the oncoming rush...softening and meeting, softening and meeting.

These moments of being fully immersed in the rushes, without turning away or resisting, took me deeper into my power, and fuller into my softness. My heart and womb, his heart, were my reference point, a place to return to after each journey of spiraling. Infinity loops and spirals emanated from here—

from form and movement into the light—connecting me to Source, to earth, to the field of love woven around us by his father and our Celestial Guides.

The intensity was building, and the forces felt greater than my body could withstand. I moved into the warm waters of the tub. The water helped me relax, and I felt held. I connected the infinity loop between my womb, heart, and third eye again. There was no turning back, for my son was wending his way down to the gate of my yoni, with the fire and fullness of his soul's desire to arrive here on earth.

As each rush came, I met it from my depths with a resounding "RAAAAAAAAAAA!" Being drawn into the downward spiral of his birth took me through more laughter, more intensity, and a brief reprieve from the overwhelming powers flowing through me.

This power was more than I could hold, be with, or channel on my own. I asked his Papa to get into the tub of water with me. Feeling his warmth and strong body behind me allowed me to melt even deeper. He was strong and loving, whispering soulful encouragements in my ear. This simple fuel was enough to gather up my strength, connect my heart again to my son, and for us all to travel the last leg of the journey together.

With the next rush, I let go of all effort and rode the wave of movement and power coursing through me. I did not push; I allowed through breath and surrendered. Not pushing meant letting go of any control, relaxing deeper into the trust of my body, his timing, and our synchronization in moving together. I reached down to my yawning yoni lips and could feel his soft head. He was almost here.

His Papa brought his hand down too, to feel him, to welcome him. two rushes later, he gently emerged into our hands, carrying all the intensity and raw power of these final moments into the water, where the intensity dissolved into peace, clarity, and contented awe.

In a few suspended moments, we lifted him from the water to the warmth of my chest. He was still in between worlds. After a few tiny coughs, the room fell silent. I gently rubbed his back. We began to sing, calling his spirit and soul into his tiny body, and he arrived with his first human breath.

We made our way to the bedroom and collapsed on the bed together to enjoy and bond with him during his "golden hour." The placenta emerged shortly afterward to be salted and coated with dried lavender and rosemary, and we brought it into our bubble of love and light on the bed. Our son was surrounded by womb mother, earth mother and father, and Love.

For two days, I nursed and rested in bed, never leaving this cocoon. His father looked after us both beautifully, bringing drinks, food, cuddles, and news from friends and family.

My initiation with my son's birth journey was surrender. Surrendering to what was presented in my life, moment by moment, showed me my deepest resistance in the places I did not trust, my darkest shadows where I would manipulate or control. Every voice within me that said no to love, no to flow, no to joy, arose to be heard. Held in the safe container of the relationship, I was able to soften and embrace these voices instead of using them as a defense. I was allowing the gentling of love.

I allowed myself to truly be seen, in my vulnerability and tenderness. For the first time in my life, I let a man support me...financially, emotionally, spiritually, and soulfully. This opened some of my deepest wounds, which could dissolve and release in the gentle harmony between us. By the time I entered my third trimester, I was open to a new degree of softness and femininity.

Just as feeling and releasing our wounds is an act of embrace and surrender, so is birth. I felt strong during the most intense rushes of birth that my 'practice' of feeling emotions arise and bringing my complete loving presence to them to release them trained me to handle the intensity of the strongest rushes opening me into bliss.

Some people call birth painful. And I did have about fifteen minutes of pain in a seven-hour-stretch of otherwise blissful, joyful, laughing 'labour'. The pain happened when I felt fear, and I let my mind run with it for a moment. When I harnessed my mind, addressed external circumstances to make myself more comfortable, communicated to Papa what was happening, and brought my full presence back into the overwhelming power of the moment, I could meet the intensity of rushes with the roar of passion, bliss, and love that I AM.

We all have moments where we doubt, when we tire, when our habit of mind kicks in and overrides deeper wisdom of presence. For me, at that moment,

I called upon the surrender that I had been cultivating for over nine months and found the way through. For me, the key was in understanding that surrendering is not passively giving in. There is an embrace and engagement with all that IS happening that takes tremendous strength.

Reflections on our Cultural Conditioning

How did one of the most sacred, blissful, and intimate initiations for a woman and her family become a scheduled, institutionalized, robotic, and traumatic event? Somewhere along the way, woman allowed herself to be stripped of the sacredness of her body. Man allowed himself to be knocked down from his innate stance as protector and soulful pillar, reducing himself to being merely a monetary provider for his family.

We gave up our intuitive wisdom and wild shamanic power to the statistical forecast of machines and the 'safe' opinions of minds in white lab coats. He surrendered the vulnerability of his vision and deep masculine presence to the grid of technology and fear.

We stuttered in the unpredictability of the unknown, letting our minds be numbed by a due date, painkillers, and a 'safe' environment. We forgot how to feel and, in fear, grasped for false safety. We lost the sovereignty and empowerment that comes from navigating the unknown and feeling into our feminine power that is unleashed from pure primordial intimacy.

He gave in to an external structure of perceived safety when he could not navigate his woman's emotional chaos. He became scared of what he could not control or understand. He aborted his mission to guide the impulse of creation into form, giving this power away because he couldn't claim it. He forgot that herein lies some of his most profound embodiment as a man through selfless action, inspired guidance, and the chance to be a true hero. We contracted and became small, subdued, and scared. He retracted and became disengaged, busy, and an observer of his own creation.

As women, birthing energy deeply anchors us into our authentic feminine power. It is rooted, circular, without doubt, powerful, expressive, sensual, and surrendered. Our feminine power enables us to meet life in all ways with transparency to be present and responsive and less reactive and fear-based. For a man, birthing energy draws forth his total presence of action, his attuned and sensitized consciousness, his joy, and his selfless movement forwards. It invokes his gentle power and grounded passion for moving him beyond the confines of what is possible. It expands his capacity to hold all that is entrusted to him in fierce protection and love. When a man is seated in this masculine power, his partner and his children can relax more deeply into the fullness of their experience of life.

Strength and surrender are aspects of love: to 'be with' 'let go' and 'take action' simultaneously. The intensity of a soulful, blissful birth gives us one of the clearest, most palpable, and direct opportunities in our lives to choose love over fear. When we call upon our strength and courage to be with and feel the intensity of sensation and emotion in birth, we arrive simultaneously in a palpable, potent presence of embrace and action. This is our innate design for birth: our initiation through birth, anchoring us deeply in our bodies and souls. Holding a field of love and total giving is the man's role, and surrender and total openness are the woman's.

Birthing is not only a practice and metaphor for how we engage with life. It is the single most impactful process on the trajectory of a human incarnation. Through my profound experience and guiding others through a journey of conscious conception, pregnancy, and birth, I became intimate with both the capacity for trauma and empowerment available to the entire family. My book, "Souls Guide to Birthing," and the doula portion of my work is a direct guide for families to use the journey of conscious birthing to heal, awaken, and discover more of their purpose and gifts to share with the world.

My platform, Technology of Love, is an in-depth embodiment program that uses spiritual science and western shadow work to open and unlock our sexuality in connection to our soul, revealing our blueprint and potential for this life. Each of our lives, as they are, brings the perfect opportunity for us to claim our learnings and our gifts. When we have done the deep inner work of making ourselves available and transparent to these experiences, we can embrace them as medicine that empowers us to truly live the fulfillment of our desires. For some, this is healing from birth trauma or sexual abuse. For others, it is claiming their life force as it organically wants to express through their desire.

Choosing love over fear is the authentic unfolding of our soul into our human experience. Our desires are the voice of our essence, longing for us into 'being human.' May we all have the courage and conviction to know the full expression of our 'being human.' that will lead to living an inspired life.

ABOUT THE AUTHOR

KATHERINE ZORENSKY

KATHERINE has guided hundreds of women and men into soul embodiment, through classical tantra and western shadow work for almost two decades. She is passionate about inspiring others to unlock the body's natural wisdom, enabling emotions to become powerful allies and cultivating the ability to transform challenges into empowered manifestations of gifts. Her current platform, 'Technology of Love,' is a combination of spiritual science, emotional alchemy, and elemental wisdom woven into a powerful method of direct realization.

Katherine has a B.A in English Literature, certified as a Rolfer, Cranial Sacral therapist, Doula, and Yoga Instructor. She ran a successful private healing practice for 15 years which gave her a depth of understanding of the body as a map into the soul. Her time living in a Zen monastery cultivated her focus, presence and mindfulness. She deepened her embodiment and understanding of classical tantra through a two year residential immersion with a Tibetan Tantric Lama. It was her daughter's birth in the Pacific Ocean that initiated her into a remembrance of the feminine path of awakening.

In 2022 she published The Souls Guide to Birthing: Handbook for a New Paradigm, a ground-breaking guide to conscious conception and birthing, combining ancient esoteric wisdom and modern practicality in the field of birth.

Connect with Katherine here:

Website: www.techoflove.com

Free 15 minute consultation: https://www.techoflove.com/connect

For all socials: https://linktr.ee/admin

SARAH TRICKER

WEAVING THE THREADS OF MAGIC FROM GROVE TO LEA

Embracing the cycles of nature breaking free from the shadows of the forest into the bright meadow

$\mathcal{A}$s a child, nighttime was the scariest. A light always had to be turned on in the hallway, shining through the crack of my open door. During the witching hour, I would stir, startled by their noise. The fear would run through me as I could not find peace. Screaming for my mother to come and save me. Looking back, I was always connected to my gift. Frivolously playing in the garden, talking with the Fae as they were kind-hearted. Those who visited at night petrified me! I couldn't understand what they wanted from me! Why me? Shadows of wolves' paws climbing my walls. Stop! Stop!

The shields are raised. Even as a young child, my mother now tells me I was around the age of five, and I somehow knew how to protect myself. Stories told by my parents about how I could close off the whole world. Their frustration as I would not tell them what I needed just stayed silent. Looking back, even now, it is clear to me, and everyone who has got close to me, that I am very internal. The need to process my thoughts, fears, and emotions is my first line of defense. Keeping things closed. No one can hurt me then!

Isn't it fascinating how focused we are now on healing the inner child? It has become a buzzword in the healing industry. As my own grandchildren are arriving in this world, I am almost envious of the tools that are available to parents today. For we each do the best we can as parents, meandering through our own tribulations at the same time aiming to make honest humans of our offspring. As you read this, you may feel that we are on a precipice of change. The healing work that is upon us is shifting our consciousness. For those who are willing to delve into their shadow, the inner child, and find their wisdom, the rewards are great.

Pathworking is a lifetime journey. The paradigms have been imprinted into us through our experiences as children. Before we can think for ourselves, we have already learnt so much from the world we have been born into. Our culture, social expectations, relationships, foods we eat, and our ancestor's knowledge. Yet, in our modern world of instant gratification, we really do expect to be able to shift things that are ingrained into our DNA and are reaffirmed by our upbringing. Why is it that we do not account for the years it took to set in motion? Humans never really seem to break the habits of lifetimes.

Universal truths have been written in history for as long as humans have discovered ways to record their life experiences. Diving into cultures and belief systems, it is clear that even before we found ways to move about our earth, the core understandings have the same threads of truth over the whole globe. If these were not universal truths, then how could almost every culture have such similar creation stories? There are mythologies that speak of great Gods and Goddesses in the sky and those who are here bound to the earth. Rituals and offerings were adhered to in all cultures based upon the shifting planets. How did we become disconnected?

Becoming a mother is a day that is imprinted into my life experience like no other. Sitting in the delivery room, I lay on the bed gazing over at the crib. My son, barely an hour old, begins to cry. I myself, only nineteen years old, have a wave of fear wash over me. I have felt this fear once before as a child at night. At that moment, I am swathed with the enormity of this precious life in my hands. From this moment forward, I am responsible. Am I enough? Yet, it was this instant that brought me closer to mother Gaia as in that moment, all of my ancestors, their hardships, and their sacrifice spiked through my veins.

Laying under the large night sky, watching the stars whilst being cradled by mother earth, listening to spirits' messages. The pain that has been inflicted by man. I feel her pain. I wonder what life used to be like for the young humans that began to discover how they could manipulate the land. Their first fire, cooked meal, the taste of food grown. Where there was no question of the feminine and the masculine. Each human had a skill, and they worked together to survive. They listened to her and learnt to live by her rules. Watching the Sun and the Moon, masculine and feminine. Leaning on the seasons to help them survive another harsh winter. Ascertaining that food can be stored, and warmth can be created. Never wasting the gifts that she provided. It was a hard life, no doubt.

Curiosity leads mankind on a path where there is no turning back. At times I reflect on the things we have available to us today. Sitting here nestled in my warm home, with the lights on, typing this chapter on my computer as the depths of winter surround me. Gazing out the window for inspiration as the snow glistens. Over many centuries mere thoughts in a person's mind through sheer determination are brought into reality. So many amazing things we now take for granted. Electricity at our fingertips, food from a store, clothing, and so many technical devices, there is never a moment where we are not plugged in.

Life is a catalogue. As you flick through the glossy pages and select the destination you desire, there are so many options. Where do you want to live? What school do you want to attend? What is your chosen career? What type of house, car, trailer, and phone do you want? What is the picture you are painting of yourself and your family? As we scroll through social media, watching the images people are showing us of their lives. With filters and staged backgrounds. Happy, everyone looks so happy.

Mental illness is rampant. How can it be when life is so easy? Is it, though? Those glossy pictures come at a cost. As people sit in their cars for two hours a day. Everyone travelling to the office at the same time. Exchanging their time for money. At the end of the month, people don't even have the luxury to spend their money how they choose as they are paying for the life they chose. Know that even those who cannot afford the glossy catalogue are buying from it. If you don't have what everyone else has then you have failed at life.

Inspiration won't be found in material belongings. A home, food, and education should be something everyone has. Abundance is not a piece of a pie that the more one person takes, the less there is for another. Our world has enough abundance for all. Each of us, as humans, living our life on the earth plane is living different paths on our soul journey. There will never be a fair distribution of wealth, health, and harmony. The law of polar opposites describes how for every positive, there is an equal negative. Here lies a key!

It is time to connect to the cycles of the earth. As we become more intelligent, we have found more ways to manipulate how we live. From Antarctica to the Bahamas, we can live comfortably in any environment. When you slow down and think about it, many countries even manipulate time. The earth spins around the sun with day and night shifting through the four seasons. Yet, we turn the clocks back and then forward. We extend the days with lights in our buildings and on our modes of transport. Is it not grandiose to think that we are not a part of the cycles of the earth? That like animals, we too, need times of rest and times of work?

Mother earth provides us with our own inner wisdom. Yet, with the spread of patriarchy, and the disconnection with the feminine, our world shifted from a place of balance to imbalance. We live in a space of duality; masculine and feminine, day and night, good and bad, healthy and unhealthy, rich and poor, and the list goes on. At the core, through society and culture, we have been taught for centuries that one is better than the other. That little boys don't cry and are tough men leaving the masculine unattached to their emotions. We don't want bossy little girls who then learn from an early age that their voice isn't worthy, eventually shying away to do as they have been told.

The rights of passage were stolen from us as the new religion spread across England. There was no one to teach us the sacredness of our bodies. Instead, as young women, magazines sold us an unrealistic image of ourselves, making us feel inadequate. As we fumbled in the dark to discover the power of our sexuality only to have it be the one thing that caused us the greatest harm. Each of you reading this today, whether you attach to your feminine or masculine energy, has a story to tell about how a part of you was taken away through the culture you live in. Sit with that experience for a while.

It is time to bring balance back to our world with the masculine and feminine, seeing it as integral to the survival of our being. That both men and women have these energies. Some men will be very masculine, some more feminine. Some women will be more feminine, and some more masculine. There will be everything in between. We need to teach our children that we need some of each within us. The Masculine represents our logic, our goal setting, our energy, and our ability to manifest what we desire in life. The feminine is our emotion, our subconscious, our shadow, our ability to connect with others, and our inner wisdom. Where do we begin?

The shadow was catching up with me. I could no longer run and hide. Standing deep in the forest, the precipice was upon me. She was calling me to listen. It was the inner child, the mother, the person I had always meant to be. I was scared; for once I shone the light bright and could see her for who she was, there would be no going back. I had the key in my hand, and the door was in front of me. To become the holder of wisdom asked me to show the world who I truly was.

They say that we are born Witches and that we only answer the calling when we are ready. Personally, it took me many years of working through my shadow to fully be authentic to who I was. The fear of persecution ran deep through my veins. My love of history started me on the path of enlightenment. As I broke the surface, a crack began to appear. I went deeper and deeper until I answered the call to teach others. In 2019, I established the Locrina Coven, and fully committed to my path. Looking back, I could not have fathomed where this path was leading me.

There was a purpose that lit a fire beneath my feet, the Coven. I could no longer find something more important to do as I planned the lunar cycles and the turning of the wheel. I gathered my years of research, tapped into the knowledge I had carried for lifetimes, and began to teach others the history. I became one of the first women in my family to fully step into our familial gift as a healer. To connect back to my history of the Cunning Folk and Druidism. Something inside of me changed.

Learn to flow with the cycle of the earth. Paying special attention to the turning of the wheel and creating Ritual for each of the Sabbats changed me in a way that I could not have expected. Before, like many, I was attached to the material gains of my work. My degrees, my career as a social studies high school teacher, my home, my new car, and all that came with it. It was crushing my spirit, and I had to escape. It was the beginning of my path to authenticity.

Money was the energy I struggled with the most. I would over plan, try to manipulate, and control how money would come to me. It would be on my mind all the time. I don't need to tell you that when I was like this, the flow stopped. On my bookcase, there are numerous books on abundance and money. All making it sound so easy, just apply this: and money will come. It didn't! In fact, the more I tried, the harder it got. What changed?

Paying attention to the lunar cycles and the season changed everything. It started simply by setting intentions under the dark moon. What did I want to work on for the next 28 days? Reviewing that on the full moon. Paying attention to the energies of the moon and how they affected me. Learning to adjust my daily ritual accordingly. This is a game-changer, my friends. It became clear that the full moon energy left me feeling lethargic, so I slept extra each morning that week. That the new moon filled me with energy, and I could easily get up at 5 a.m. and work harder through this week. The biggest ah-ha moment came from giving thanks for the turning of the wheel. It was so blindingly obvious I couldn't honestly believe I hadn't noticed it before. Humans are like the earth and all its animals that live amongst us; we need to hibernate in the winter too. We have gotten so used to high functioning seven days a week for 52 weeks of the year that we don't allow time to rest properly. If we do rest; well, you're lazy! We are consuming everywhere that only people who work 16 hours a day are successful. Well, I am here to tell you otherwise!

A well-rested mind increases creativity and productivity. My whole being started to shift as I prepared and gave thanks for each of the Sabbats. From the spring through to the winter, the equinox to the solstice. The story of the Goddess and the fight of the Holly and Oak King. These are the stories that show how we need both feminine and masculine to bring balance. The seed and the womb bring an abundance of food. The importance of returning to the underworld for rest and contemplation. I no longer feel the need to push through the winter, fretfully aiming to complete tasks. After the harvest and Samhain, I prepare for the time to rest. I allow more sleep in my daily ritual and spend more time reading or relaxing in the evening. When I released the guilt and allowed my body to follow its designed cycle, I felt like a million dollars. Spring arrives, and I am clear of mind with creativity running rampant through my veins. I finally found balance.

This was only part of the journey. You know when people say "trust the universe has your back." I don't know about you, but I believe that definitely takes some time to admit. It wasn't that long ago that I had some lessons show up for me. In 2019, I had one of the biggest years of expansion in my business. It felt like I had finally reached my dream. I had moved into a 3700-square-foot building on the main street and had two staff members, and over 30 women registered in my year-long programs. Yet, some strange things had been showing up. Every time I did a reading for others, the Tower card would fall out. Every time I shoved it back into the deck, thinking that's odd. I also had this urge to wear one of my new pendulums as a necklace. Hindsight!

Well along came 2020. Things started to feel different right at the start of the year. The Tower Tarot card forewarns of an unseen change that can manifest as crisis, destruction, and yet liberation, let me tell you the message was hitting me loud and clear![Ma5] The energy was somehow shifting. People started dropping out of my programs, and staff began to turn against me; in just a few weeks, my whole world was coming crashing around me.

I have this newfound faith that everything does happen for a reason. After some deep conversations with my hubby, the decision was made. If I could cover the store rent for February, I would keep the store open; if I couldn't, the store would close. I would have to move my business home. I'm sure you have guessed it, I couldn't cover the rent. It all fell into place as this was the end of my six-month contract and then the pandemic! The] whole world was shifting.

The darkness surrounded me like when I was a child. It was time to go within and heal. Heal the fact my dream had gone. Heal the mistakes I had made. Heal the losses I had experienced. The store closing, I believe, was divine intervention. Wow, am I glad that I had already learnt to listen to the cycles. I could see when it was time to let go. My life purpose was still clear; I knew what I needed to fight for. I now must take women through the journey, weaving the threads of magic from Grove to Lea so they, too, can embrace the cycles of nature breaking free from the shadows of the forest into the bright meadow. The understanding that perseverance is most important. It is true when they say it takes twenty years to become an overnight success. I now fully trust the journey and do not focus solely on the destination. F***ck, the destination can change in an instant!

Hold on to your uniqueness! We live in a space where we seem to be in constant competition with everyone around us. This takes us right back to material wealth. Abundance is so much more than your belongings. My inspired living and hope for you is to be able to live with gratitude for each day that you are gifted in this life. To step outside in the rain, snow, or sunshine and connect with the currency of mother earth. Knowing that there will be both ebbs and flows within your life. Be at peace when the ebbs appear and be willing to dig deeper into your shadow than you thought possible. When you get there, bring the balance of the light to shine bright. Embracing the shadow as it too is a part of you. You no longer have to push the shadow away. Like the nurturing of a seed in the womb space, it needs time in the dark before being born into this world.

"Life by design." You may think I am lucky as I forge through creating a way to live my life purpose. Stop! Stop comparing! Stop comparing yourself to anyone but you. Where did you start, and where do you stand now? Each of our soul's purposes is so vastly different we cannot even compare. It is time to bring balance back onto the earth and our lives. Where the feminine has a place at the table, and so does the masculine. That we are empowered to heal the mother wound. With each generation of womb healing, we are forever changing the footprints of this earth. When we are the ancestors, we know we forged a path of greatness. It is time to connect with our ancestor's wisdom by connecting with our own. Today, I give you permission to stop searching outside of yourself. It is safe to look within. "You are enough - and you alone - hold the power to be uniquely you!"

ABOUT THE AUTHOR

SARAH TRICKER

Be enchanted, motivated, and feel the magic! SARAH, the founder of Sarah Tricker Alchemy, is a healer. She has created rituals to empower women who are struggling to find their authenticity and life purpose. Sarah is a non-conformist who forges her clients ahead to think bigger. Every moment is a miracle which is within every woman's reach as she embraces her feminine power.

A fifth generation Medium, Sarah has spent a lifetime working with Spirit. Moving from the public system as a teacher Sarah has now created her own Academy. Her passion to teach women to connect with their inner wisdom. In 2021 Sarah was awarded Rookie of the Year in Toastmasters. She was also handpicked in the Brainz CREA Global Awards.

With a passion for lifelong learning, Sarah holds a B. A and B.Ed, is a certified life coach, Reiki Master, Medium, and Yoga Teacher. She is also a Senior Executive Contributor for Brainz Magazine. As an alternative holistic healer, Sarah is centered on finding many modalities to support her soul contracts.

Sarah is a mother of two, a wife, and a Nana. She is an English soul that has found her place in a rural town in Southern Alberta, Canada.

Connect with Sarah Tricker Alchemy

Website: https://sarahtrickeralchemy.com

Comp session: https://sarahtrickeralchemy/limitedoffer

(Discover where in your life cycle you are at, to take your power back)

All Socials: https://sarahtrickeralchemy.com/biography/

NINA ACOSTA

TRANSCEND YOUR LIGHT

REDEFINE YOUR REALITY

I remember the first time I realized I was connected with a divine knowing. I could feel the powerful energetic force internally and out in the world—It's one of the same. I recognized it as an energetic frequency more powerful, beautiful, and majestic than anyone can distinctly fathom.

As children, we are so resilient, connected to God, and in tune with all the beauty the universe has to offer then years of conditioning make us forget how truly loved and supported we are. And before I take you on this journey, I invite you to: take a moment, close your eyes and remember the resilient, loving, fearless, spiritual being that you were created to be and connect with that child. Hug, hold, laugh, play with your inner child and let them know that everything is going to be just fine. Your life is happening for you—not to you. You're always loved and supported by a powerful, unconditionally loving, energetic frequency that I like to refer to as *God*.

The vibrations from the bombs and guns fired in the distance would put me to sleep. For protection, the military mandated us to stay inside and sleep on the floor. It was ongoing for several months, but the war did not seem to bother me as a child, although I'm sure it has affected my worldview on some level. I remember seeing helicopters, soldiers, and gorillas from time to time since we lived so close to the jungle in Panama. *But I also remember not being scared.* Eventually, we were told we might need to evacuate and only to pack one bag of our most treasured items. So, I asked my mother, "If we die, will we all be in Heaven together?" Not having a concept of what or where Heaven was, I was comforted by her response. My inner being felt the potency of the unconditional love this angelic realm provides. I knew I was supported and unconditionally loved, and whatever happened, I was fearless because of my unwavering trust and connection. You see—my "inner child" was intuitively connected; I was born to be divine—and I carried God within while embodying trust and fearlessness because of my internal knowing. I brought that distinct knowing with me until the conditioning of the world began to set in; then, I forgot how truly loved and connected I really was, and some may refer to this phenomenon as adulthood.

I was living a life on auto-pilot, survival mode, with self-inflicted pain and suffering. I always took the path with the most resistance—that was me in a nutshell. I don't really recommend this; you want to take the path of least resistance. Just saying from experience, but if you're an experiential learner like me, well, I love you and love yourself through the lessons! I continued to walk a self-destructive path, lit the match, burned bridges, and dropped bombs on my own life. I laughed, cried, grieved, screamed, and prayed while my life unraveled right before my eyes. I used sex, abusive relationships and friendships, drugs, food, and everything in-between as coping mechanisms, simply because I didn't want to deal with the internal war within my mind and soul. I lived a life of divulging in the ordinary existence of my creation, bored out of my mind, and unintentionally creating chaos, so I was feeding my false belief of unworthiness. I also wanted to be accepted by society and loved with conditions because I didn't think there was any other way. Until one day, three decades later, I became inspired to claim my birthright as a powerful co-creator by embracing my connection, intuition, the wounded, the healed, the unique, the weird layers that made me beautiful. I, finally, was ready to do the deep soul work, learn new techniques and tools to help facilitate my healing process, and invite my inner child to come out and play. I was able to change my life.

'Inspired' is such a beautiful word with different meanings depending on who you are and your worldview. Even in the darkest of times, there is always love and inspiration; you just have to connect to it. What I have found is that: throughout my darkest moments in life, the divine never leaves you. I mean, how can it be since it's inside of you? The divine loving, energetic frequency is waiting for you to connect and receive it. It's always working for your highest good! Finally, my inspiration came to me after decades of pain, repeated patterns, spiraling from past trauma, and emotional highs and lows. My dominant frequency, the vibration I was used to operating in, was low. I didn't feel worthy of the life I wanted to create, love, abundance, wealth, or anything in between. I have always known I had a purpose, but I didn't want to explore it because I was sure my ideas were much better. It wasn't until I finally threw up my hands because I was figuratively hitting my head against a brick wall. I thought to myself; there has to be more to life than this? The same situations kept manifesting in my life, repeatedly with different people. I recognized the pattern, but I was not connecting the dots, which created the life I wanted to run away from.

I was living in a low vibrational masculine energy. Take action, execute, get shit done, go-go-go mentality. I was then shaming myself for working long hours, not taking care of myself, and missing time with my son. My body was starting to shut down. I was anxious, forgetful, tired, exhausted, getting sick all the time, entertaining toxic friendships and connections, and occasionally fainting. I could no longer operate at this low vibrational masculine energy. In hindsight, I realized my vibrational frequency was leveling up. My low vibrational masculine energy was moving to a higher frequency, and my feminine energy was making itself known. However, at the moment, I didn't feel that way.

Then, I had a thought, what if life could be different? I know God created life to be abundant. Why isn't it working for me? What if I'm responsible for all lessons that kept showing up? What if there's truth to creating your reality? In this reflective moment, I was inspired to think differently. I knew I needed to ask for spiritual help. I called upon God and my helpers to show me a sign. I was tired of running away from my purpose. I was tired of the internal fight within my soul. My soul knew I was awakening, but my human self could not logically grasp what the heck was going on. I was upleveling my consciousness. The inspiration in that very moment led to a deep soul dive of unraveling my most authentic self. The thoughts I pulled from a collective consciousness inspired me to make a choice; I did not want to continue to live the life I created. So, I started to let go and asked for signs, which led to the manifestation of a free onsite 3-day retreat with spiritual practitioners. Still, to this day, I remember the moment when my phone rang and the event coordinator told me that my fees had been waived and that all I needed to do was cover my flight. I laughed to myself in disbelief; I thought it was a joke, but it wasn't a joke. It was divine intervention. When God or the universe gives a sign, we are responsible for acting upon it and letting go of the outcome. In retrospect, that is exactly what I did. If I let go of "hows" and "ifs"; it would eventually happen. I trusted that if it was meant to be, God and the universe would work out all the details.

Inspiration will come to you in many forms, thoughts, dreams, words, songs, signs, and nature is just a few ways. It's because of the lack of faith in God, the universe, that so many people struggle with living the life they desire. We are designed to live a life full of abundance. We were made in his image, which means God lives within us. There's a strong correlation between being connected to God and yourself (who God created you to be). We, humans, hop on the struggle bus of living an abundant life because society conditioned us, since the day we are born, to be everyone except who God created us to be. We are conditioned by our relationships, interactions, the media, environments, and generational trauma to be everyone but our most authentic selves. Think about it? We pick vocations, marry, lovers, occupations, friends, neighbors, etc., based on who we "think" we are rather than who we truly are. It's a strange yet normal phenomenon. It's more common to live a life on autopilot than to live an abundant life. As I choose the path less traveled, I step into my power and create a life I desire. As I continue to travel on this journey, I realize I am already abundant. Abundance is a frequency, and I already have everything I could ask for. The rest? They were just icing in the cannoli!

My journey is still not complete, but it's never about the destination, right? I'm day-by-day shifting and changing because I made the conscious decision to choose growth. And I will always choose growth for the highest good. Why the highest good of all? When we heal, we heal others and heal the world. I can tell you from experience that your reality is created by how you feel internally. You will keep attracting what you do not want if you do not get clarity on what it is you want out of life. I transformed my life from living in fear and avoiding shadow work to leaning into lessons and feeling joy no matter the circumstances in my 3D reality. You may be asking what changed? How did I get to the space of internal peace? How did I quit spiraling? How did I quiet my mind and eliminate my anxiety?

I Started Choosing Myself

I'm still a work in progress, *but I had to take extreme ownership of the life I created and start dismantling it.* I began forgiving myself for the choices I made in the past. I didn't realize until I began to heal that I had emotions of guilt, shame, and anger, dancing around in my subconscious mind. All of which were attached to situations that happened decades ago. How did I know? I started living in the present. I slowed down and controlled my breath, using different breathwork techniques. Then I would ask myself where the thought or emotion came from. Is it mine? Is that true all the time? Most of the time, I realized the negative emotion or thought I was feeling wasn't even mine.

I remember the moment it all came to a head. I was in the midst of a relationship, one of those perplexing ones. We're friends, not friends, and more than friends, among other things. This was going on and off for a couple of decades. If you have ever found yourself in this type of relationship, you know exactly what I am talking about. No judgment; we have all had them from time to time. It happens to the best of us. What I realized is that every time I was with this person, I felt less than myself. I wasn't good enough because of how I perceived their actions. Regardless of their actions, I was choosing that type of relationship, and I was choosing those emotions. It seems like a small moment, but it was the catalyst. The relationship came to an end. Later, I realized he was my mirror for all the wounds inside of me. All my relationships up to this point were the same—my lack of self-worth, my closed-off heart, fear of being seen, vulnerability, and connection. He was mirroring back exactly how I felt on the inside. More importantly, I kept reliving the same patterns in our relationship, just like I kept reliving the same patterns and lessons in my life. There was a parallel in my life, and relationships were filled with polarizing emotions because that's exactly how I was showing up to the world daily.

Open mindedness Leads to Insight

So, let's fast forward back to the retreat, you know, the free retreat I mentioned earlier. The retreat was on sacred land in Dolores, Colorado, through a community called Authentic Living by Mandy Morris. It was only for a few days, but it was the best investment I have ever made. I've gone to counseling and hired coaches, but I have never experienced anything like this in my entire life. I've never visited a land that felt so loving and supportive. I mean, it's still weird to hear myself say that, but it's so true. I was one of those closeted spiritual people that spent most of their time in their logical mind, but something is very different about the Heartland; it's life-changing. Although I knew I needed help, I didn't know what to expect. I was still kind of skeptical but enjoyed the cozy quarters and spectacular vegan cuisines. I promised myself that I would keep an open mind. I mean, there was a reason why I was there. I asked God for help, and this is how it showed up in my life, so I followed my intuition. I was determined to show up for myself. At this point, I had nothing to lose. I'm so grateful that I stepped outside of my comfort zone. While I was there and long after the retreat, I was still experiencing energetic shifts, and my mindset was constantly evolving. I took ownership that I was contributing to and creating the toxic behaviors in my relationships and life because of my fears. I recreated the emotional highs and lows because of the unhealed traumas in my life, and it was my way of life. However, I knew, that after this retreat, my life was never going to be the same—in a beautiful and abundant way!

Upon my return, I was intrigued. I knew I had to learn how Mandy creates these lasting shifts, so I immediately dived in to learn her techniques because now, I was on a mission to heal, serve, end generational trauma, and create a life aligned with my soul. As I continued to heal, I eventually became a Love and Authenticity Practitioner; this methodology uses Science, Psychology, and our divine connection to All That Is. My experience was a beautiful awakening; it was like an unveiling. My perspective of the world shifted dramatically. I had beautiful awareness that the internal war I was battling was all in my mind: my thoughts, emotions, lack of confidence, and self-care routine. It was derived from not embracing all of myself and dimming my light to make others feel comfortable. Up until the retreat, I've done a lot of personal development, but I was not implementing what I've learned. You see, we all have the power to change, but you have to do it for yourself. You have to want it badly enough to do whatever it takes. Sometimes, that means temporarily distancing yourself from your loved ones, and it can also mean letting go of relationships that you intuitively know are dimming your light and learning to hold space for yourself.

Clarity will Lead to Creation

I love being a coach; I love serving my clients and watching their shifts and transformations. I want to be clear. All my clients have the answers inside of them. I'm just the guide that challenges their perspective and provides them with the concepts and tools to make a lasting transformation. These are the same techniques I use in my life to keep getting into flow and keep the inspiration going. The funny thing about coaching is that you seem to attract people who resonate with your energy and, sometimes, because of your lessons. To truly make a lasting shift, you need to build clarity on what you want to create. Is it a loving relationship? A prosperous business? An empire? An abundant life? Success? Is it all of the above? We all have different worldviews, and these concepts have different meanings for everyone. So, what is it that you truly want? And who are you authentically? Once we see things from a clearer perspective, God and the universe will divinely supports us.

I have worked with both men and women, and one common theme is being disconnected from God, the universe, and the self. When I listen to my clients, they are conditioned (as we all are) to be fearful of becoming who they are authentically created to be. They have a deep fear of being seen, vulnerable, and loss of connection or judgment. As we go through our process, I hold space for unconditional love because I serve as my higher self. I see them for who they truly are. I teach them the same methodologies I learned and use daily. I teach them how to protect their energy, daily check-ins of their emotions, energy, thoughts, morning routines, self-care, reconnect with God and self, forgiveness, and everything in between. Sometimes, it's the practical techniques we use on a daily basis that leads to the macro shifts. It's the compounding interest of becoming 1 percent better every day that leads to the transformation.

So, when your soul chooses to awaken, remember that life is not happening to you. It's the beginning of your journey to self-mastery; it's a synchronicity of all the good life has to offer. I feel we, humans, make life seem way more complicated than it needs to be. It's simple, we only have one life to live. Why not live it? Why not figure out your authentic self and what you really want out of life? Why not seek peace? The choice is yours, and the world is your oyster. Why not create heaven on earth? Not only for yourself, but for me, and for us.

ABOUT THE AUTHOR

NINA ACOSTA

NINA ACOSTA is the founder of Transcend the Light. As a certified Love & Authenticity Practitioner, she helps women step into their power and create a life they truly desire! Her methodology combines psychology, science, and the woo-woo. Her deepest desire is to guide others to rediscover their most authentic self!

She believes the key to creating the bad a** life you love, starts with being connected to God/Source, the core of your purpose, and what you stand for! She teaches women to reconnect with their voice, power, and most authentic selves. Her mission in life is to uplevel consciousness because when we heal ourselves, we heal others, and heal the world. For you, for me, for us. If you're interested in collaborating with Nina, she has an offer for everyone, simply connect!

Nina has been featured in the *C-Word Magazine*, *Elephant Journal*, the *Be Ruthless Podcast* and *Art for Wellness Podcast*. She is a contributing author to *Inspired Living* and the *Faces of Mental Illness, Anxiety*.

Connect with Nina here:

Website: www.transcendthelight.com

Freebie: https://bit.ly/freeclaritysesh

All socials and connections: https://linktr.ee/ninaacosta

STEPHANIE O'CONNELL

MY QUEST FOR FLOW AND AUTHENTICITY

Where did my Inspiration go?

I was sipping my morning coffee during a rare quiet moment and started reflecting on the state of things in my life. I had moved to a new city for a fantastic leadership position in a well-known company; my husband had landed the architecture role he most desired, and our twins were in the public middle school, making friends and adjusting well. We found a house that needed some repair but worked for us in the location we desired. All seemed good on the outside; however, I was troubled on the inside.

What was I feeling? The first three feelings that surfaced were stressed, conflicted, and depleted. I took another sip of coffee. "When did my life become so stressed?" I looked back over the last couple of years, and the days were a blur of work deadlines, the twin's school activities, household maintenance and repairs, and family commitments. I seemed to be running to and from things constantly–and then waiting. Waiting for things to begin or finish so we could run to the next thing. My husband and I communicated as needed on the tactics of the day to get things completed. We also did the regular dance of adjusting when the unexpected happened. Both of us had demanding jobs and so we were constantly comparing our commitments to see which ones were the most critical ones to meet on that day. There were days when I felt I could not win. There always seemed to be a trade-off to make. No wonder I was feeling conflicted and depleted. "What else am I feeling?" I asked. I got quiet and felt a dense heaviness in my heart. A sense that my life had become uninspiring and unfulfilling. A photograph from my college days filled my mind. The photo showed a version of me that was joyful and ALIVE. A version of myself that was determined to break free from my alcoholic environment and the family dynamics I had experienced. A version of myself that was ready to prosper and thrive in the world. A version of me that was passionate about helping others learn and grow. Where did my inspiration go? I then felt a deep sense of loss because, at that moment, I realized I had lost my way. I had stopped listening to my heart and followed the beat of another's drum. I had become disconnected from my soul and so my day today lacked purpose and passion. I sighed deeply. I knew at that moment something needed to change. With this awareness, I set out on a quest to reconnect with my heart and soul.

The Quest

I started reading and researching ways to be authentic while aligning with my soul purpose. I was clearly not alone in this quest, as there were hundreds of articles, books, and courses with perspectives on authenticity and purpose. I began to wonder, "Why do we lose connection with ourselves?" and "How did it happen to me?"

Growing up, I remember having a sense of "inner knowing" about things. I would say things and just know them to be true. When I got to school, my teachers told me that "knowing" was not enough. One needs to "prove" what you know with facts, figures, and data. I thought about the times as a young adult when I listened and followed my intuition. In those moments, I had a steadfast trust and belief that the choice was "right" for me. I felt light and energized. Then I looked at the times when I did the opposite of what my intuition was saying. In those situations, I felt stressed and conflicted. I felt obligated to make that choice at the time. That is an example of when the expectations of others influenced me to override my intuition. I noticed that something similar was happening at work. I observed myself holding back my thoughts, ideas, and perspectives time and time again I would give myself pep talks: "Be courageous," and "Speak your Truth." Why was this so hard for me to do? Why did it feel so risky? I realized that the voices around me from family, school, and work were gaining influence in my life. I started following this external flow of expectations and rules to live by instead of following my own flow. Why? I wanted to be accepted and belong. I wanted to "fit in" and be a team player. I wanted a successful career and financial stability. I thought that to climb the corporate ladder, I needed to think and act a certain way, and in some companies, that was true. I learned the rules of engagement. However, the higher I climbed, the more stress I felt. The pace of the work was relentless, and days blurred into weeks blurred into months. I was so focused on work that I had lost sight of other aspects of life. I had a successful career but was deeply unhappy.

Returning Home

"Why was climbing the corporate ladder so important to me?" To answer this question, I journeyed back to my childhood to get a clearer picture of how those early years shaped my beliefs and behaviors.

My childhood environment was filled with emotional, social, and financial insecurities. To survive, I created and adopted a set of beliefs to keep me safe. One set of beliefs focused on pleasing and getting approval from others. I learned quickly that when I pleased others and did what they expected, life was easier. I learned to bite my tongue and disregard what I wanted to ensure I pleased others. I was very good at it. I believed that if people could depend on me to support their needs, then I would have the emotional, social and financial security I craved in my life. I also saw how hard my mom worked as a nurse to keep the house running and how my Dad struggled to keep employment. I developed a belief that in order to earn money, you had to sacrifice other things in life. Looking back now, I can see clearly how I developed a fierce independence "I will do it myself" and why I was so driven to succeed. I also saw the cycle of addiction and codependency all around me, as well as why "people-pleasing seemed to be my path to peace at the moment.

With this awareness, I reviewed the decisions and choices I had made in friendships, and I recalled many times that I would not share my truth with friends for fear of upsetting them or bothering them. I recalled times in my marriage when I did the same. I found myself making excuses for not speaking my truth. I would think things like, "oh, don't bother sharing that idea; he already knows what he wants to do anyway." I had lost touch with my true needs, wants, and desires while playing the role of "wife". The effort it took to play the business leader role, mom role, and wife role was exhausting. My husband and I were no longer aligned mentally, emotionally, and spiritually. We started to drift further and further away from each other. Then something unexpected happened, and everything changed.

My husband suffered a near-fatal heart attack while at an outdoor retreat. He was flown by helicopter to the nearest hospital with a cardiac surgeon. He survived the heart surgery and has had a full recovery. But the heart attack was a wake-up call for both of us. Life is uncertain, and both of us were unhappy. We realized that we had grown apart, and our marriage was no longer working for us. We talked about reconciling, and both felt that it was best to end the marriage. We started having real candid conversations and developed a plan to divorce and raise our twins together as supportive co-parents. Even though we mutually agreed to divorce, it was hard to face the fact that the marriage had failed. It was an emotional time, and I personally felt the cost of living an unaligned and uninspired life.

I am not proud that my marriage ended, and I certainly made my share of mistakes. I needed to heal to move forward. Awareness of my own needs was an essential first step in my healing and growth. I now needed to find healthier ways to get my needs met. I learned methods to rewire the neural pathways in my mind, so the cry of fears became a distant echo in my mind. I learned to transmute my lower-level feelings of shame, guilt, and anger into more elevated feelings, and I retrained myself to listen and follow the flow of my intuition. I use all of these proven practices in my coaching and healing business today.

I met mentors that resonated with me. I went on retreats and became a love and authenticity coach and Geo Love energy healer. I went through a rapid process of assessing my beliefs and feelings and worked on lovingly releasing the ones that no longer served me. I realized that the corporate leader role I was doing was not aligned with my soul purpose. My role was eliminated during a company restructuring, so I decided to step off the corporate ladder and start my own business. I was scared and excited to take this big leap and design a life that was more balanced and integrated. I learned to trust and believe that through love–all things are possible. I opened my heart, and magic started to happen. My relationships elevated, and the ones that did not elevate any longer affected me in a negative way. I reconnected with a dear friend from college, and we both fell deeply in love with one another. I established new ways of interacting with my family. This was when I started to understand and appreciate that when I make joy a priority, brilliant ideas come naturally, support surrounds me, and good things come easily to me. I realize now that leading with my heart and following *my* flow is the best way for me to live an inspired and joyful life.

Dream Bigger

I have been in the field of organizational learning & development for over 30 years and have led large-scale corporate transformations. In my experience, the more successful changes have a positive, intentional energy that fuels the change efforts. An example of positive, intentional energy is "We are changing to bring more solutions to our customers." While "We are changing because the business is suffering great losses" is fear-based intentional energy. It is very hard to change when we are experiencing fear.

I have coached hundreds of business leaders on how to lead change and empower teams to deliver. These leaders take care of business while also taking care of people's hearts. Tapping into the emotions surrounding the change is essential for lasting change. We can all change to comply; however, this type of change is short-lived. The positive change acceleration method I developed leverages positive, intentional energy, alignment principles, and fast action. I use business change practices, coaching, and energy work to "make change happen".

Let's Begin Changing Right Now. Think back on your last year and quickly reflect on the changes that have occurred during the past 12 months. Some of those changes were probably things you chose, while others were probably things over which you had no control over. But you *did* change!

The truth is that we tend to underestimate how much we can grow, heal, learn, accomplish, and manifest in a year.

So, in order to begin the process of accelerating positive change in your life and bringing in more changes that you do want, I invite you to imagine yourself a year from now and reflect on the following questions.

How do you want to feel?

What do you want to have in your life?

What do you want *more* of? And what do you want *less* of a year from now?

What kind of people are you surrounded with daily?

In what ways are you embodying your purpose?

How ready are you to change?

Journal on these questions as much as you wish.

Make sure not to overthink your answers — let them flow to you from a place of pure desire.

And know that anything your heart desires is possible.

Then once you're done, put the paper you wrote on into a box or an envelope and set a reminder in your calendar to look at it exactly a year from now. Think of it as a reminder of how you have manifested positive change in your life—in one year.

This is a powerful exercise because we underestimate what we can accomplish in just one year! And nothing is impossible, especially when you surround yourself with people who support you and provide you with the right tools at the right time.

I invite you to get so connected to your own inner truth and talents that when you open that letter a year from now, you'll think, *"oh, I guess I need to dream bigger."*

Perhaps you don't want to wait one year. With our fast-changing world, you may be in a place where you need to process the forced change that has happened to you, or perhaps you realize that you need to initiate change in order to avoid a rude wake-up call in the future. Either way, I invite you to join my free masterclass and discover Your Roadmap to Heart-Centered Change. (Find the registration link in the biography).

My current photos show the version of me that is joyful and ALIVE. Every day, I encourage you to connect with your heart and soul so that you can flow with inspiration, joy, and love. It is worth it!

ABOUT THE AUTHOR

STEPHANIE O'CONNELL

STEPHANIE O'CONNELL is the Founder of Positive Change Acceleration LLC, an intuitive Change Acceleration Coach, an accomplished Energy Healer, and seasoned Fortune 500 Organization and Leadership Development Corporate Leader. She is passionate about change and transition and encouraging individuals to consciously live and lead across all dimensions of their life. Her practice combines change philosophy, coaching, and energy work to facilitate and accelerate desired change. Her proven methodology has helped individuals, groups, and organizations undergoing any form of transition accelerate their journey and reach their fullest potential.

With over 30 years of Corporate Leadership, a background in communication, leadership, organization development and theater, Stephanie is a Mastermind Mentor, Authenticity Coach, and Master Energy Healer.

Stephanie holds a BS in Communication Studies, an MS in Organization Development, is a certified MBTI professional, Love and Authenticity Practitioner, and Geo Love Energy level 3 healer.

Stephanie currently lives in Milwaukee, Wisconsin USA with 3 generations in her home and two lovely dogs named Zelda and Penny.

Connect with Stephanie here:

Website: https://www.positivechangeacceleration.com/

Book-Bonus: https://www.positivechangeacceleration.com/book-bonus

For all socials and to book a call: https://linktr.ee/stephanie.o

PART III

UNLEASHING CREATIVITY

SAMANTHA LOUISE

THE DEVIL RETURNED ME TO GOD

F**ck! It's happening again. Thank God I caught myself before it was too late this time. I can't afford any more days lying in bed, crying, paralyzed, pleading for the pain to end.

I can't afford it... I can't stand it... I refuse to be controlled any longer. When I spiral, the fear inside of me takes over. The darkness hits and drags me down in an attempt to stifle me. I'm still ashamed when it happens. As if I don't have the self-control or the power over my own thinking. The triggering process is like an attack on my senses—coming from places I cannot predict: a scent, a story, a laugh, a song.

But I hold out hope. I have learned that it's not just me that falls into the abysmal pit of life-shattering hopelessness. A place that you can only fathom if you have been there yourself. Because of this, I don't tell many about it. I make up stories about why I might have to cancel a meeting, ask for an extension in a project, or even request a raincheck.

Although the darkness and pain destroy me at times, I recognize the beautiful gifts of self-discovery and personal growth that emerged through the challenge. The most private chapter of my life prevails as the most empowering and transformational. My inspired life required the learnings of this journey.

You see, growing up, I was accustomed to the Midwestern culture of tough, hard-working, rural, conservative European descendants. Here, emotions have no place. Actually, there are a few in need to perpetuate the facade of control and authority; anger, rage, passive-aggressiveness, and shame are welcomed warmly.

I'm smart and learned at an early age that my creativity, mind, body, curiosity, and presence were too much for most people to accept as inspiration for a new way to live in joy and in purpose. The grooming process began, and I learned to bite my tongue when irritated, keep my wild ideas to myself, and never burn a bridge even if it led to harm, manipulation, or abuse.

My body developed much earlier than the other girls my age, and I realized that if nothing about my authentic self was valued, at least my body might be. In teenhood, the urge to compete and be the best took hold, and it lasted well into young adulthood.

Who could I show superiority over? What skill could I learn and assert to show my worth as the best of the best? Athletics. Academics. Arts. Cooking. Marriage. Work. Men. Alcohol. The list grew until, one day, I woke up and didn't want to fight anymore. Proving my worth through achievement took its toll, and I gave up.

Yet, as my spiritual journey began, I thought I was perfecting it and flowing freely. Yoga. Meditation. Mindfulness. In the desire to grow and be better— I binged videos, books, and teachings of contemplative practices from cultures around the world and through history. My intuition told me I was onto something and to keep seeking more knowledge and wisdom from the best.

When I discovered his work, the existential questions I struggled to answer about my life suddenly fell together like puzzle pieces, slowly and naturally creating a detailed picture of me and my life experiences. Each lesson helped me make more sense and begin to distance myself from the cultural rules that bound me to an antiquated life.

As the learning process grew deeper and accelerated, the boundaries of a student-mentor relationship blurred. He saw power and beauty in me that he wanted all for himself. For me, the seduction of an elevated lifestyle drew me to trust—to surrender; to be taken.

Anything I wished to learn, he could teach. Any challenging relationships I had with friends were eliminated. Toxic workplace environments vanished, and I prepared to build an international business, poised as a leading expert in women's empowerment.

Eventually, I began to sense a more profound change within myself. It seemed like I was *coming home* to a part of myself I never knew. What I believed to be my personal truth washed away, replaced by a more sophisticated life purpose. Value and belief systems that grounded me in service and leadership morphed into a righteous calling.

I thought the profound changes would also illuminate greater opportunity and reflect higher levels of success in all aspects of my life—this is what my initial spiritual training taught me. Yet, the more I gave in to the new lessons, the less joy, achievement, creativity, connection, and love I felt inside. I grew alarmed, hyper-vigilant, and scared.

Darkness flashed amidst the false luminescence that originally dazzled and mesmerized me. A voice from nowhere, always present, steadfast, remained part of this journey. To Hell and back, I danced, I sang, I broke bread, and even laid with the Devil. Intoxicating. Tantric. Sensual. My senses overwhelmed - the darkness overtook me. And I couldn't find my voice to say, "No."

Suffocating. Screaming. Searching for my soul and my life, the hand of an angel appeared. As if on cue, it seemed to listen, grieve, guide, and love me. Now, a neutral heart carved out space to hear my stories and begin to ask simple questions about my needs. It helped me reground and paint a picture of the current reality.

I found myself on cloud nine during the good moments. But during the manipulation, confusion, and arguments, I began to spin. Only submission and obedience stopped it. On the darkest of nights, I planned my escape to run as fast and as far as I could. Determination more fervent than the Devil's temptations guided me to reprieve.

In a physical space more than a house, a spiritual retreat, the angel's soul had embraced me to be hidden in plain sight. Only through the eyes of an angel could the damage, erosion, confusion, and detachment from self be seen. With the strength of an army, I was protected by God's Angel wearing the body of a man.

Healing ensued, but the Devil kept knocking, luring me back regardless of the fear and anxiety. I learned to function in the panicked states of being. I was playing my cards right to keep the Angel at bay and please the Devil. Discernment is a powerful tool, and I realized the intuition of the Angel could see through the lies.

My greatest fear of being abandoned grew. Ironically, the still strong voice within remained intact, and the Angel's words grew firmer, more focused, and sweeter. I reached the lowest point of my life and decided this was the moment. My escape plan was still in motion, and finally, the reclamation of my own power and voice prevailed.

No! No more bullshit. Life! This is my life. Love! I must embody real love.

I took my life back. God, where was God? I had to speak with Him and learned I could find him nearby. A place on Earth where God walks with humans - exceptional humans. The hermits. Those of us who seek isolation on the journey of self-discovery during our pilgrimage to best fulfill God's calling.

I asked that the Angel deliver me to this sanctuary, a safe space untouched and unharmed by the Devil. Prepared to face my own demons, I entered a state of sheer joy and serenity. Peace overcame my senses, my mind, and my soul in the hand-off. An Angel delivered me to God? Yes. This place is Heaven on Earth. Pacem in Terris.

This retreat offered nourishment, truth, and light as the only resources on-hand to heal and move deeper into my inspired purpose. I learned it is in quietude and nothingness where the soul is called home to reconnect with God and set ablaze the path of destiny. So, I entered the silence to be alone, completely trusting the process of prayerful inquiry to receive whispers of wisdom.

The Devil returned me to God. My power and beauty: too much to handle. The light within me might reveal secrets kept in the dark. I no longer have the urge to explore the darkness. Life in the lightless cavern of my former self afforded me the tools to navigate adversity and chaos so that I might share it with others.

Now, for the Angel, a gift of thanks was in order. Money? Food? Hugs? Adventure? No. He requested nothing more than the simple gift of authenticity. For me to return to my former self wasn't an option. In a moment of truth, I jumped into a free fall of faith, knowing that who I am meant to be will only emerge through courageous action.

The Angel seeks what he so freely gives. I learned to use the mirror to see in myself what I see in others as beauty, honor, love, strength, and greatness. When I turn away in disbelief, I plant my feet, breathe, and come back to my mind-body in the present moment to take up space in this world that is rightfully mine.

Finally, I am here. I am home. See me now. Hear me now. I am a mysterious, teachable warrior. A poustiniki on a pilgrimage, my voice is finally full. And I bring an invitation for other fallen warriors to return to Light. I call out for you to take my hand, accept support, and discover your authentic self by shedding your faults, pain, and old self-beliefs. Step into your best life of inspiration and creativity.

God loves us. Angels stand with us. Light leads our way. No anger, wrath, punishment, or shame rains on you in a life of compassion, grace, and love. Really, you can love and be loved. So please, come home, my sisters. Do you feel unseen? Set your sights on the greatness within you. Do you feel unheard? Tune your ears to your inner voice.

The journey starts within. External triggers will force you to go deeper. Only the brave-hearted accept the challenge to face the darkness and end the cycles of generational dysfunction, rewrite the unwritten rules of culture, and dissolve the disturbingly unrealistic expectations of society. I believe you are called on the journey.

Marking the onset of my next chapter in life, I vow to live by the values and beliefs that honor my personal needs. Through vulnerability, I seek justice to make right the wrongdoings, injustices, and suppression of girls and women to live in freedom and the pursuit of a life of joy.

This is my testament that God is alive and well, walking among us with Angels every day. When the heart turns away from good due to disbelief and disillusionment, wounds and pain must be examined and healed to become balanced, whole, and well, perhaps for the first time ever.

I'll guide you gently, shed light at your feet, and reacquaint you to self-love if you are afraid. You know the way home, sisters. Your higher self awaits your arrival, honoring your journey, hearing your stories, and embracing your wisdom. There is a spot at the table for you, a leader with a vision. Now is your turn to own your excellence.

Come home to activate your creative life force energy. Be free to live in peace.

ABOUT THE AUTHOR

SAMANTHA LOUISE

SAMANTHA LOUISE is a leadership cultivator guiding girls and young women to become natural born leaders. She is an author, a Minnesota Teacher of the Year, and holds a Master's degree in Educational Leadership. Her approach to leadership and learning offers hands-on experiences to develop selfhood for self-leadership, sisterhood for healthy relationships, and leaderhood to inspire change in the world around us.

Every workshop, retreat, and lesson offered by Samantha incorporates whole person wellbeing, cultural mind-body science, and interfaith spiritual practices. *The Devil Returned Me to God* is a story calling women back to their true essence and personal truth to thrive after detrimental people pleasing, unhealthy relationships, and dysfunctional belief systems.

Samantha has been featured on such popular podcasts as She's Invincible, The Influential Woman, and The Rhonda Grant Show to discuss demasculinizing women, healing through vulnerable justice, and new perspectives on leadership. From a farm in rural America, Samantha is a small-town girl with a world-wide vision to transform leadership development and personal empowerment for next generation female leaders from every corner of the globe.

Connect with Smantha here:

Website: https://www.samanthalouise.co

Freebie: Meditation & Journal
https://www.samanthalouise.co/inspiredliving

More: https://linktr.ee/samanthalouise.co

JACINE GREENWOOD

UNLEASHING CREATIVITY

I grew up in a household full of creatives. My father, despite being a priest, had been a musician in a past life and could also paint incredibly well. My brother could not only draw but also paint and write his own music. My sister could paint and be good at poetry. She also hand-made all my niece's very intricate ballet costumes, complete with lots of sequins and beads. Then there was me, who couldn't do any of those things. The best I could do was cook. I always looked at creative people with awe because it was one of the things, I thought was my weakest gift, yet it ended up being my strongest one---with me going on to win awards for my formulation skills as a cosmetic chemist.

My family is either just intuitive or gifted, with my mother being able to speak in tongues and see angels; my sister being able to see inside bodies, and my nephew able to see things. Again, I felt like this gift had skipped me altogether. My intuitive side, however, did not reveal itself till I was around 36 years of age.

As a child, I was always told I was lucky. Everything just fell into my lap with little effort on my edge, and I never realised why. I just asked the question, "How?". How can I get this? How can this happen? I think I had done it instinctively from childhood. In my mind, nothing was impossible, especially when I really desired something. We grew up with not a lot of money, and so I would fantasise about all the things I desired. Pretending I had them already. I did not realise at that time I was using the law of attraction or that I would become a master of manifesting.

Around the age of 36, I started getting answers to my questions from the universe. I would ask specifically for my cosmetic formulas and what I needed to do. Initially, I questioned the messages I was being given. So, the universe showed me more than once in one day until I suddenly realised what I was being guided and told. When I first started developing my formulas, it was completely from a science and logic perspective; however, as I began to unlock my intuition, I was often given the knowledge of bizarre herbs that I had never heard of. I was shocked when I researched further to find these plants had a long history of medicinal use in ancient cultures and actually had documented evidence of their efficacy. I started listening and taking notice of what my intuition was telling me, and my formulas became known for delivering results.

One time I created a product for an Indian woman who had an autoimmune disorder that not only affected her eyesight but resulted in skin rashes occurring as well. We had tried her on our current products, and it wasn't helping at all. I decided to create a formula for her that would specifically address the skin rashes. The new cream not only got rid of the skin rash but also lightened her skin. I was shocked and couldn't believe it. Now, at the time, I had a vision board with the statement "I created a solution for melasma." I did not even realise that I had until she told me. This cream was then adapted for one of our professional in-clinic treatments. I have found that guidance doesn't always come directly. And often, discoveries are found indirectly and almost by pure chance and accident. Although my belief is there is no such thing as an accident, it is alignment.

Initially, in business, I kept this side of me hidden. As I had become known within the industry for my science knowledge, I was unsure how this other side of me would be received. I was worried about losing credibility and respect, so I tried to keep it hidden, but it wouldn't let me. My intuition speaks to me through a massive, uncontrollable shiver. It comes when I least expect it to affirm me that what I was thinking or what was spoken is correct or true.

Hiding my secret became pretty impossible when you do a massive shiver in front of a room of people who you are teaching. It would literally stop the room, and someone would always ask, "What was that? ". I would have to use my guidance system, also known as intuition, to respond. My "shiver" became famous with them waiting to see if their words struck a chord in me and elicited a response from my body. It is how I choose ingredients, and all my suppliers have seen me and understand what it means. If I am reading something and my body responds, they automatically know that I need a sample of that ingredient and further information. They don't even ask if I want it anymore. The shivers didn't happen just with my own words or thoughts; they also happened with other people as well.

Over time as my business grew, I became less afraid of what anyone else thought, and so I started showing my true colours. The more I let the "real" me be revealed, the more of a following I attracted—with those who were already following me falling in love even more with who I was and what I represented.

My staff also learnt to trust my intuition as there were predictions of growth that I "just knew what was about to happen." When asked why I thought it would happen, I couldn't answer. It was more of a knowing. I tried to explain it as though it was an energetic phenomenon. I could sense energy building up, and a tension that was driving me and pushing me, and I always listened to it because it had never been wrong.

By attracting more and more people, I realised how much potential I had to inspire them. For the past five years, I've said that my only wish is to inspire people. Inspire them to keep dreaming. Encourage them to pursue their dreams. Motivate them to keep going. To fan the flame of hope within them so that they may find their true destiny and the gift that they are meant to bring forth to the world. So many people give up on their dreams. I am not sure if it is because they think it is easy or because they are comparing themselves to others.

Comparison and Social Pressure

Comparison has and always will be the thief of joy. I know my own journey had been a long and arduous one, and during this time, there had been numerous times I wanted to quit—but I didn't. I kept going because there was a calling and something bigger than me, which is why I continued.

Inspiration to me means living in alignment with who you are and allowing you to bring your gifts to the world fully. To be fully able to play in your genius zone for the majority of your day, rather than doing tasks that you don't enjoy and that someone else does better. When we are living by our true purpose and vision, even when we are working, we don't feel like we are. Inspiration makes us open to possibilities and is the doorway to creativity.

One of the biggest hindrances for people truly living a life of inspiration is cultural, familial, and societal pressure to fit into a "mold" of what is expected. Families with a history of academia are particularly pressured into a career path that may not suit what the person truly enjoys. My own son had felt pressure to pursue a path in Engineering from his father. Only after he realised that it was okay to change paths did he choose Graphic Design instead. A path that he is much happier on and unleashes his creative side in a way he could never have achieved with Engineering. Sometimes we put these pressures on ourselves because we don't want to disappoint our parents. My son was afraid I would be disappointed. I couldn't have been prouder of him for his decision. He chose something that he loved instead of doing something that he did not enjoy. As I told him, "If you love what you do, then you cannot help but become a master of it."

Collaboration is a Dance of Energies

It is my belief that we are not on this earth to do things alone and that, as a community, we can achieve far more. Often as entrepreneurs or business owners, it can sometimes feel like we are competing with others. And that if, somehow, someone else succeeds, there will be insufficient for us. This, however, could not be further from the truth. The idea of collaboration or joint ventures is not utilised anywhere near as much as it could be in business. Joint ventures or collaborations are a win/win scenario for both parties.

When I first started in business, I was very open and receptive. I freely shared a lot of information about why I did it, what I did, and the ingredients I used. I did this until I got burnt by a customer who literally tried to duplicate my product. I was devastated when it happened. I stopped trusting so much and became a lot more secretive. After that experience, I withdrew and was not so open with information and sharing. It took me a long time to realise that I could still be open but hold information back so that I didn't give away my secrets.

I had been asked numerous times if I would privately label my brand and had always refused as I had spent a long time growing my brand reputation. Private labelling is when someone purchases your product, adds their own branding and labeling, and sells it as their own. Our results were well-known, and if I allowed a customer to private label under their own branding, there was a good chance they would use our Roccoco photos to promote their own brand label. It was a possibility that they would reveal it was Roccoco, but at a cheaper price point. It also risked us losing our current clients and customers, so I always had said no.

Have you ever held on tightly to something for fear of losing it? Have you noticed how that actually contracts your energy and denies you greater creative expression, expansion, and abundance?

I had never considered creating anything outside of Roccoco that would also be desirable. But over the past 12 months, I opened to the possibility of contract manufacturing for a large company, which would be worth millions to me. This potential contract was the beginning of my door being open to creating skin and hair care products for other people. We developed three products for a company at an affordable price point. The products were nothing like my brand but served a gap in the market the customer was looking for. It also allowed us to fully use our equipment, which had previously been inactive for weeks at a time, depending on when we were making that particular product again.

If I am not Creating, I am Dying

At the time, my team asked me to slow down product launches because the amount of work in marketing and graphic design was considerable, and they were struggling to keep up with the workload. This used to frustrate me so much as I had so many ideas of what I could do, and I wanted to bring them to life. The challenge was: How? How could I still unleash my creativity without burdening my creative team more? Creativity was everything to me. I would say to my staff, "If I am not creating, I am dying." That is how strongly I felt about it. Every time I would learn about a new ingredient, I would get so excited, only to be followed by disappointment because I knew that the team would protest if I wanted to bring out another product.

I realised that making products for other people was a way for me to fully embody my creativity. It allowed me the joyful process of research and creation; it just happened to be for somebody else. I started getting referrals from people who knew me, hoping I could help their friends or acquaintances develop some products for them to sell under their own brand names. My reputation as a formulating chemist was growing. Each inquiry made me excited as an opportunity for me to bring my creativity to life through someone else.

Vision Boards

One of the processes that I have used to allow creativity to come alive is the use of vision boards as a daily practice. I have utilised vision boards for not only the development of my creations but also in other areas of my life, such as relationships, health, and wealth. The way I was initially taught to do vision boards never worked for me. I was always told to find images of the life I wanted and stick them on a cardboard sheet or use something like Pinterest to form a collage of images of my ideal life. I also struggled to keep my images to what I could fit on a piece of cardboard. I could never get excited by this and struggled to bring emotion up when I looked at it.

I realised, after I did Neuro-Linguistic Programming, that vision boards may work for visual people; however, visual was my least used method of sorting information. I mainly used auditory or sound, which explained why I loved music so much. I found adding music brought my vision board to life literally for me emotionally. I changed the way I did things. Instead of using a static image on a sheet of paper or Pinterest board, I decided I needed it to be like a movie, and the images needed to be moving so I wasn't starting at the same image all the time.

I started using my vision board for the goals of products I wanted to make, putting down what I had created and the results that it delivered. I was amazed when I actually started bringing them to my life literally before my eyes. The goals on my vision board were pie in the sky and lofty, and I had no clue how they would come into existence. However, the continual watching of them impressed my subconscious many times that my subconscious brought them into existence.

The process of being open has resulted in me now having several clients for whom I am custom-creating products. It also opened up the possibility of developing my own private label range and allowed me to fully express myself and live in an inspired state without having to put pressure on my creative team. I no longer viewed others who wanted a brand as competition. Instead, it was a collaboration because as they succeeded, so did I.

Learning to trust my intuition and allowing myself to fully embrace my creative side has given me freedom and happiness that is unimaginable if you have not experienced it. The ability to create is life force itself and generates even more energy within me. My clients who are contract manufacturing love working with me as we create something unique to them that has a massive 'wow' factor, which they are looking for. It allows for a collaboration of minds where we both celebrate wins.

As I reflect on my career this far and wonder how I have managed to become so successful, I put it down to these factors:

1. Taking inspired action on my intuitive hits.
2. Finding a way to keep expressing the creativity that moves through me by finding new business models to do that.
3. Creating win-win situations with others through collaboration instead of wallowing in competition.
4. Understanding the power of programming the subconscious mind through vision boards
5. Allowing my unconscious mind to determine priorities of what needs to be done.

How could you unleash your creativity? Where are you holding back and still giving in to the pressures of society? What inner voices do you still need to release to unleash your spirit free and step into a life filled with inspiration?

I put the success I have been blessed with down to the unleashing of my creative spirit. It has expanded my business beyond my wildest dreams. And—it is my desire for you that you may do the same.

ABOUT THE AUTHOR

JACINE GREENWOOD

JACINE GREENWOOD is a best-selling author and award-winning Cosmetic Chemist. Nicknamed by her customers as "The Fairy Godmother of Skin", she is well known for solving skin issues that leave even the most experienced dermatologists baffled. Her mission is to inspire and give hope back to her customers.

With over 25 years' experience, she has helped thousands of people achieve skin they have only dreamed about and is regularly sought out by consumers who have been left with absolutely no hope of a solution to their skin issues. With dermatologists referring to her as "The Skin Girl", her formulas have won numerous awards and she is well known professionally in the industry for her innovation and outstanding results. She is a regular guest speaker at conferences and writes for professional journals within the cosmetic industry.

In 2021, Jacine was named in the *Australian Financial* and in 2022 in *The Financial Times,* because she is the fastest growing beauty brand in the Asia-Pacific Region. Her business, Roccoco Botanicals, grew from her kitchen sink into a multi-million-dollar business. She achieved this whilst having had chronic pain and five spinal surgeries with fusions. This created an unstoppable mindset and extreme resilience. She now also coaches business owners how to grow and scale their business rapidly with no money spent on advertising.

Connect with Jacine here:

Website - https://www.jgdcoaching.com/

Freebie - https://www.jgdcoaching.com/bonus-download

Linktree - https://linktr.ee/jgd_coaching

DR. ANN BARNET

INSPIRATION REVIVED ME

This is a story for anyone who has been shunned, ostracized, or excluded because of an illness. A look back at navigating the terrors of COVID by finding hope and inspiration from the previous generations who healed from leprosy. Learn why many people shut out those who are sick and what we can all do to come together and overcome fear through love and acceptance.

An out-of-focus video showed a man walking down a sidewalk in China. He stumbled and then fell over dead. This was the moment COVID violently grabbed my attention. A slew of similar videos followed. Soon, there were images being broadcast of chaotic emergency rooms in New York City with uneasy crowds and ambulances being turned away. Bodies were shown piling up in a parking lot in Madrid.

I felt a heaviness in my stomach as country after country was shut down, and we were told to 'go into lockdown'. Do not leave the house unless you have a medical emergency or need food. If you do leave the house, avoid others at all costs. Do not breathe the air that others have breathed. Do not touch anyone.

As those first waves of COVID deaths hit the shores of the United States, I was working as a doctor at the hospital where I was born. We had been understaffed for months leading up to the pandemic. More than half of the physicians at our hospital had recently left due to contract disputes. Many of us had been covering extra shifts to fill the gap. I had just finished working twelve-hour shifts for twenty-one grueling days straight. I was exhausted and numb. Covid arrived, and I was asked to give even more.

I did not know how I would be able to care for others, as I could barely care for myself during those early days. To me, the hospital felt like a contaminated nuclear power plant. We did not have the personal protective equipment we needed. One person at a time, we were admitted into the auditorium to receive one single-use N95 mask. It was only given to me after I carefully signed my name, and I was checked off the list. I was instructed to use the same mask for the next ten days. Then we had a conference call where we were given vague information from the Center for Disease Control. The most obvious question came up first, "Are you really suggesting that we reuse a contaminated mask?" The task force leader mumbled, "umm...yes", his voice audibly shaking. One of the senior critical care experts suggested, "Up in the ICU, we've been cleaning our masks with the hospital-grade disinfectant wipes." I replied, "The ones in the purple containers that have the warning to avoid contact with your skin as they are highly toxic? " I panicked. We were screwed.

I immediately ran to the liquor store and bought as much high-proof vodka as I could find. I then braved the stunned masses at Walmart, where most of the shelves were already empty. I bought as many small spray bottles as I could find. I went back to my kitchen and made a non-toxic solution of 75% alcohol and a few essential oils to mask the odor. I poured them into the bottles with care. 'This is a safe disinfectant; this can help,' I reasoned. The next day, I took them to the ICU. I offered some to the doctor in charge on that particular day. "Oh Ann, that's cute," he said condescendingly. "I'll stick with what I'm using." I was shocked, but his words left no doubt in my mind. I could find no one here who was thinking clearly. I had no choice. I had to find the voice of inner wisdom and "knowing" deep within. It was the only guide I could trust.

I went home and spent the majority of the next few days curled up in the fetal position. Severe vertigo washed over me each time I tried to open my eyes. I could only crawl a few inches before feeling overcome with the sensation that I would fall. The room was spinning, like one of those teacup rides at Disneyland.

Unable to do anything else, I meditated. I accepted that complete stillness was my only option, and I allowed myself to fall through that nauseating portal of fear. My only movements were my breath and enough steps to make it to the sink, where I managed to drink a few sips of water.

Our Deepest Fear

I was in a dark and lonely pit of fear. I had heard stories of others who had been here before.

The deepest fear that a human carries within is the fear of being alone, cast out, and isolated from their tribe. In the early days of humanity, isolation equated to death. This was a theme introduced to me by my father when I was very young, and he has been a great inspiration for all of my work. My dad completed his medical training in the late 1950s. He had a deep calling to help the marginalized and traumatized. Having just returned from the army, where he had been stationed as a doctor at a hospital in post-Nazi Germany, he learned of Father Joe, an Italian priest with a vision to build a clinic for lepers in a place called Northern Rhodesia, now known as Zambia. Leprosy was a gruesome disease. It left its victims blind, with their fingers and hands falling off in large pieces. It had been lurking in the shadows, stalking humanity since pre-biblical times.

Those who suffered from the disease were loathed and dreaded. Anyone who was affected was immediately outcast and deemed "unclean". They were expelled from their communities and families. For centuries, this stigma persisted. Small communities of afflicted people formed; some were banished to isolated islands. By the nineteen hundreds, lepers were still shunned by society. However, because there was limited world news at the time and no social media, they were mostly ignored and forgotten.

When they arrived in Zambia, there was no cure for leprosy. Yes, there were a few remedies and medicines that helped temporarily, but the fear and cruel disfigurement continued to cause much suffering. "How did you do it?' I asked my father. "Weren't you afraid?". He said, "No, I was not afraid of leprosy. I was afraid of the crocodiles. The worst thing I saw there were the three women who were killed by a crocodile. He nearly devoured the first woman, and the other two were mangled when they tried to save her. All three of them bled to death. It was gruesome. There was nothing I could do to help them."

Covid has, to some degree, given many of each of us the experience of being a leper. Because of fear, many wonderful people were shunned. People were shut out or excluded themselves because they were told that they were dangerous and unclean - a threat to others. Soon the experience rapidly expanded further than the unseen viral particles could. Once a vaccine was introduced, it seemed as if all hell had broken loose. People were still dying alone, but now the pain was compounded by name-calling, public shaming, and threats. People became increasingly polarized. I struggled with this. During my time as a doctor, I have taken care of hundreds of patients who have refused treatments. I shared with them my advice and then accepted their decisions, out of autonomy even when I did not agree. But any conversation about vaccinations had become taboo. If I wanted to discuss this, I had to be prepared to lose my job, my reputation, and even my friendships. When I finally built up the courage to speak, I was met with some support. I was surprised that the most common reaction to my questions was a deafening silence. It was isolating.

When the lepers were expelled from their towns and villages, they needed to find a way to survive. They did. First and foremost, it was mother nature who provided for them. They foraged for food and eventually started farming. They found allies and companionship among the other lepers who had also been cast aside. Some had family members who refused to alienate them, even if it meant a great risk to themselves. So, they formed their own communities. After some time had passed, people eager to help, like my father, became involved. In the early 1970s, a cure for leprosy was finally discovered. It consisted of a combination of three antibiotics given for a prolonged period of time.

The exile was understandable in the sense that the disease caused horrifying damage. Leprosy was poorly understood. There were numerous misconceptions about how it was transmitted. Although it is actually spread through prolonged and close contact with respiratory particles, it was widely believed to be transmitted easily. You would, of course, want to protect yourself and your family. Caution was required; however, the extreme degree of isolation was inappropriate and cruel. The lepers were still humans and they had needs. They deserved healing and compassion.

Looking back, it is clear that healing in that leprosy colony began long before those antibiotics arrived; even long before my dad and Father Joe appeared.

Love and community are rooted at the core of all healing. They displaced the fear and paved the road to redemption. It took hundreds of years, but the fear of leprosy gradually faded, and lepers have now been reintegrated into society.

Reclaiming Power

COVID offered me an invitation to discover what it would take to dissolve my own fears. I came to know that my journey was not to overcome fear but rather to find the treasure that lay beneath it. The terror controlled my reactions at first, but then I remembered that my mission was to *show up, be present and be of service* in this life. Steadfast in this knowledge, I was able to take action. The stories of leprosy touched me. It gave me the hope and unshakable belief that healing on a global level is possible, regardless of what I was hearing from the media.

When I finally emerged from my cocoon of panic, I felt calm and resolved. I wondered if this was how it felt to be at war. Knowing that you were walking into what felt like a certain danger but compelled to carry on. After all, this is what I had signed up for. I had spent a decade of medical training, sleepless nights, and spiritual work preparing for this. My father had been in a similar situation. He did it without even flinching. When Covid arrived, he was ninety years old, and more than anything, he wanted to go into the hospitals and help. So, I borrowed some of his courage and enthusiasm. I recognized the privilege of being a doctor and the honor of having a defined mission. I took a deep breath, and I drove through the deserted streets to the hospital.

At least the hospital and its covid wards were a familiar place, as I had walked these halls and entered the rooms of the sick and contagious thousands of times before. Strangely, I quickly felt ok. Surely, I had already been exposed to the virus, and I was fine.

I may have been feeling better, but my patients were terrified. It's normal for people to be afraid when they are admitted to the hospital, but what I saw was another level of fear.

My first covid patient to die was the father of an ICU nurse. She had been working at another hospital, and she was guilt-ridden with the belief that she had infected him. She begged to see him. She had her own PPE equipment and knew the protocols, yet she was not allowed to enter his room. I was so angry I could feel my heart pounding in my chest; the pressure building in my head. Five minutes after he died, she was asked to come to collect his belongings. She was escorted through the contaminated halls and handed a bag. How was it okay for her to be in the hallway but not in his room during his last minutes? I was as furious, and she was devastated. These decisions made no sense.

Luckily, I had more control at my own clinic, where we could provide alternative treatments other than those available at the hospital. At first, we provided care in the parking lot in people's cars, so the infection did not spread inside. I could not stop smiling as I witnessed patient after patient improving. None of our patients, even those who were initially struggling, needed to go to the hospital. I attempted to introduce some of the vitamin and mineral-based treatments that had proven effective at the clinic into the covid treatment plan at the hospital. Unfortunately, they were not approved. This only inspired my partner and me to share the solutions we had found, and we launched a small nutraceutical line.

I spent a few days buzzing with anger and resentment until I decided to channel my energy in a more productive way. There were some good things that were happening at the hospital, and despite my frustrations with the covid treatment plans, I wanted to stay. I felt that my presence there was needed more than ever. I realized that there were other things I could do at the hospital. The most immediate intervention was to help the terrified patients release some of their fear. "Turn off the news". That simple action was powerful. The relief on their faces was remarkable, and patient after patient told me, "You're right, the news was making me more upset."

Information is valuable. However, being constantly bombarded by horrifying images of worse-case nightmare scenarios is toxic to the body, mind, and soul. The body needs to feel safe in order to heal. Blood and resources are literally diverted from the job of healing and repairing the body when we are in a state of extreme fear. I introduced my patients to the mindfulness practice Emotional Freedom Technique to help our nervous systems shift from a state of fear to a state of calm and repair. This is a simple but effective practice that resets the primitive fear centers of our brain. It can be used as a manual override to let our nervous system know that we are safe and that it's okay to use energy to heal. The simplest version is to place your hand on your heart, take the biggest breath you have taken all day and then exhale slowly, making a sound as you do. Now, gently tap on your heart, the same way you would comfort a crying child. Send that part of you that is afraid and overwhelmed with thoughts of love and comfort.

Soon I was using this technique on myself to move through my next layer of fear. The initial terror had morphed into fear of carrying the virus. I was concerned that I would have no symptoms myself but might pass it on to people I love or my most vulnerable patients. This fear of harming others took the longest to come to terms with.

I recall the day when it shifted. Over a year into the pandemic, a friend who had been living close to the land and removed from the media invited me to a small outdoor gathering to celebrate his birthday. Indigenous elders had traveled there to pray and celebrate life. People around me were not afraid. They were alive, treating each other how humans are meant to treat one another. Some even hugged each other. For lack of a better term, it attuned my nervous system to a frequency of safety. The heaviness lifted, and my body truly relaxed for the first time in months. I was reminded how much we need to be with other people and to celebrate.

I continued to take precautions, especially when in the hospital. However, my paranoia was gone, and I was able to help my patients more. Then the medical journals started to publish some reassuring studies. Contrary to what we were told in the beginning, the data suggested that it is very unlikely for an asymptomatic carrier to pass the virus on to others.

Stress Stops all Logic

Humans have no control over how they respond to fear; it is a programmed response. I came to understand that the polarization and rejection were not personal. The more evolved area of our brain that processes language and makes decisions is also shut down by fear. Good people shun other good people out of fear. Brilliant people, stop thinking clearly when they are afraid. For me, this knowledge made it easier to forgive both myself and others. Covid placed us all in a collective state of fear. This includes those in positions of authority. As angry and frustrated as I was, I recognized that I had to let it go.

There are ways to override the fear response, and it usually requires outside help. When someone is frozen in fear, simply being in the presence of someone whose nervous system is calm dissolves the fear. Perhaps that is why our most fundamental fear as humans is being kicked out of the tribe and excommunicated. Another being who is not in a state of fear can effortlessly broadcast that safety is nearby. This is often an unconscious transmission. "I feel peace close by, I am safe here."

We can also melt into fear. Completely. To feel that which we imagined was too uncomfortable to feel and to recognize that we are separate from that feeling.

This sometimes happens in meditation- we can separate into the being that is experiencing our lives and the being that is observing us in our experience.

Love and Inspiration Revive

We can all find that still point in our being that allows something else to wash over us. That something else is acceptance and love. This is what heals our fear. This is the starting point for all true healing. This happened to me when I was curled up into a little ball at the start of covid when inspiration revived me. It also consciously reconnected me to my purpose. I looked within and drew strength from my greatest source of inspiration. I had to. Without inspiration, what was the point? What did I have to give me hope? I needed my father's reminder that no matter how bleak and hopeless the world seemed, there was always a way out.

The leprosy colony that my father helped start still stands today. I went back with him to visit a few years ago. He had the most touching reunion with the last remaining leper, Gabriel. He had been my father's guide decades earlier. Gabriel could not see them through his clouded white eyes, but tears of joy rolled down my father's face as they embraced. We all walked through the cabbage fields and up to the building where they had worked together. Inside, patients were still lined up on benches. Rather than lepers, the patients were now women about to give birth. The place that was once a colony for lepers is now called the St. Francis Mission, and the community there cares for babies and pregnant women. It remains a welcoming refuge, a place full of laughter and life. It may have taken decades, but the shame has been washed away. The Saint Frances Mission is a reminder to me and so many others that even if an illness causes you to suffer alone in desperation, there is always hope.

ABOUT THE AUTHOR

DR. ANN BARNET

DR. ANN BARNET is a physician, adventurer, professor, student, entrepreneur, humanitarian and most importantly a lover of nature. She practices both Hospitalist Medicine and Integrative Medicine, focusing on balancing the multi-faceted fundamentals of health and living a well-balanced and joyful life of purpose.

Ann has great respect for indigenous traditions, having been influenced by indigenous wisdom while studying in Bolivia and serving in the Peace Corps in West Africa. She works with several amazing partners that focus on providing healthy local food to regional communities. She also provides medical care at numerous festivals and independent events.

As the co-founder of a nutraceutical company Lig and Ceptor, she constantly learns from nature in her pursuit to integrate holistic knowledge with traditional western medicine.

Connect with Ann here:

All contact details: https://linktr.ee/annbarnet

Subscribe to her newsletter to win the raffle: https://ligandceptor.com/pages/contact

Subscribe to her newsletter, filled with valuable tips and you will be entered to win a special gift basket that will support your health! Drawing for the winner will take place on July 27, 2022.

HABEN DELALLATA

INTRINSIC KNOWING

THE SECRET TO UNLEASHING THE WILD WOMAN WITHIN

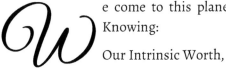 e come to this planet with 3 Intrinsic spheres of Inner Knowing:

Our Intrinsic Worth,

Our Intrinsic Individuality, and

Our Intrinsic Wholeness.

These three things are part of us, just as we are all part of each other and the Universe. And we Must Explore each of these areas to Unleash the Wild Woman Within.

Our Intrinsic Worth comes from knowing we are valued, loved, and cared for by Something Greater than us. I call this God; when I say 'God,' I mean the collective of both Heavenly Mother and Father, our Savior, the Angels that walk among us, as well as those who have gone on before us, and anyone else genuinely invested in our success.

It doesn't matter to me how you quantify GOD, "knowing" who we are and who we come from helps us feel a sense of Great Worth, and nothing can diminish us.

Our Intrinsic Individuality has been called many things, such as autonomy or sovereignty. All that means is that we come here with self-determination. We come here with innate likes and dislikes. We arrive with an inner "knowing" of who we want to be and with an internal compass—our heart—telling us the best way to get there. And when we listen and honor that inner "knowing," we Stand in our Power!

Living, in our Highest Expression, is the best thing we can do for ourselves and others. To me, this means finding out what makes your Heart Sing with Gratitude and then Do More of That! You will be Happier, and You will make the World a Better Place *JUST* by You Being You!

Our Intrinsic Wholeness means we "know" we are part of something larger than just me and you. Everything we do has an impact on the world around us. We are not an island. Humans were created for and are strongest as a community. We desire to make connections in relationships and build families. We want to nurture and safeguard those bonds. This is why the universe has our back—because everything is connected. So if you win, so do I! You could even say that competition is an illusion because there is *MORE THAN ENOUGH* to go around and take care of ALL of us. It's just a matter of perspective and alignment.

All three of these things are intuitively known to us. And all it takes for you to access this intrinsic "knowing" at a deeper level is a safe space and a meditative state.

Then get Curious!

Ask Questions.

Lean into the Answers,

And see where they take you!

Every Single Time I do this, I experience more Joy, more Peace, and more Ease!

Wild and Free

If you knew my mom, you would begin to understand why I am who I am. My mom has this quality about her; it's regal and fine, yet daring and free! Her Trust in God runs deep, but she is also Fiercely Independent.

I came into this world full of *daring and an innate desire to do things my way.* Some would have even called me *Wild*, not an unintelligent sort of wild, more like UNTAMED!

As I was writing this chapter for you, my mom told me that not only was I given freedom during the most formative years of my life, but she had planned my childhood to be that way.

You see, my older sister, who's a beautiful redhead, regrettably grew up in the late 60s and early 70s. Not a friendly time to be a kid. And if you were a kid and *thought* you could get away with flying under the bully's radar, well, you could forget it as a redhead! Red hair, even today, draws attention like a bull's eye, eliciting all kinds of unwanted attention from others, making my sister's childhood a living hell. My mom witnessed all this and saw how it affected my sister. This made my mom determined to create a safe space for her next child to grow up in. So she started making plans for a simpler life.

By the time I was born, my mom had moved from a big city in Texas to a small farming community in Iowa. Here, she cultivated a rich childhood for me, unmolested by the outside world and its damaging influences. My sister was thirteen by then, so in many ways, I was an only child. I was surrounded by adults who loved and doted on me. But adults have lots of boring adult things to do, so I spent a lot of time alone playing and exploring with my imagination. It was a *Golden Time* for me; I'm certain I walked and talked with God every day. I'm so grateful that my mom gave me that freedom; it anchored inside of me a self-knowing that NOTHING has been able to completely extinguish. My mother, more than anyone else on the planet, exemplifies the type of woman I aspire to be. Her Faith in God and Autonomy center and ground me.

However, I must have been lonely as a child because I LOVED meeting new people. But with all of my freedom came isolation from the outside world, which meant there was very little need for instruction on how to behave in public. I *didn't* know there were social rules, and that people *don't like it* when you break those rules. Since I spent most of my time with adults, I was exuberantly excited and completely enchanted when I met another child. This must have been a lot for other more socially groomed children because I quickly learned that not everyone liked me back.

In the woods, I felt at home. I was confident in who I was, but kids were different. They didn't always say what they meant or behave in predictable ways. And I didn't understand why they didn't like me as much as I liked them. It confused me because I was Awesome!

At least that's what I thought... but maybe I wasn't!

What *if* it was *ME* that was the problem?

The Game

That poisonous thought planted itself inside my mind at a VERY young age.

When I experienced other peoples' disapproval of my behavior, I didn't have CONTEXT, so I took it as though it was *ME* that they disapproved of. And that thought lived very comfortably inside my mind for over 3 decades. It grew deep, penetrating roots that twisted and choked my self-confidence. Soon it had even grown a voice that snarled and tore at me. Every hurt, every misunderstanding, strengthened its hold on me. And its voice slowly grew louder with every sting I perceived. It skewed my vision of myself and others. Soon I was looking at the world through the lens of *I'm Not Good Enough*. And if I'm not good enough, then that means I'm not lovable, and I will be rejected and eventually die. Sounds dramatic, doesn't it? But children depend completely on others for their safety and well-being. So I learned how to do everything I could to MAKE people Like me.

This, as you can imagine, isn't an easy game to learn. The rules are constantly changing, and not everyone plays fair. But I got really good at reading people. I was smart and quick, so this technique helped me survive most of my life. But it came with a heavy price; each compromise I made to feel safe and accepted quieted that Wild Child inside a little further. The more I tried to fit in, the worse I felt about myself—which made me try even harder, because I *didn't know* it was *The GAME* that was wrong, I BELIEVED it was ME! This led to an insatiable need for attention and approval, but nothing I did could fill that void BECAUSE it was a LIE! I was not the problem, but its the only thing that made sense to me at the time. We all do this. We all look at the world through distorted lenses, and we all have a version of this Game in which we hide.

Smoke and Mirrors

By the time I was fourteen, I was *so* lost in the Game that I had no idea who I was, and I couldn't recognize myself in the mirror as anything but a threat. I hated practically everything about myself. The constant fear of rejection had taken its toll.

I had gone from a vibrant, thriving child; to a depressed teenager, desperate to find a way to feel good about herself. *But* that desperation led me to search for God in earnest. I needed to know that God was REAL and that I Mattered to Him! I knew if there was ANYONE who could teach me "How to Be Happy," it would be God. As a child, God was one of those intrinsic inner knowings. But as a teenager, I needed something more concrete. So I began searching for Him in the lives of my friends. Many of them claimed to know God, but I didn't see Strong evidence of Him until I went to visit my aunt in Texas.

At that time, we lived in Tennessee, and it was the summer of my freshman year. My mom told my aunt how concerned she was for me, and my Aunt was like, "We'll take her!" And so I got on a plane for the first time in my life, and I flew to Texas.

My Aunt was a member of The Church of Jesus Christ of Latter-Day Saints. I had never heard of that religion before, but as soon as I started studying with the missionaries, I *"KNEW"* I was Finally HOME!!! It was as if I started remembering myself again; as if the smoke and the fun mirrors that I'd been scrutinizing myself in for so long began to lose their power.

The missionaries taught about Heavenly Parents who love us and want us to experience Joy! They taught about families being sealed together forever. My Aunt's family and my new church family helped me understand the significance of having a Savior. And the more I understood the character of God, the better I understood myself. I was given a completely new way to see and experience the world, and I loved exploring it.

What I Really Needed... was to feel Safe

That was also the year that I met Bryan, the love of my life. It is not lost on me that as soon as I began to repair my relationship with myself and reconnect with God; I was also aligned with my Forever *PERSON*.

When I first met Bryan, I was highly enjoying my freedom; so I wasn't looking for anything serious. But it didn't bother him because he wasn't in a hurry! He "knew" what he wanted, and he had the confidence and the patience to wait for me to figure myself out. His quiet confidence intrigued me. He was the first person, besides my mom, to really See and Love me for ME. This both scared and irritated me. By the end of our 10th grade school year, before I went back home to Tennessee, he told me he had feelings for me. He told me, and then he let it be. And so I went back home, back to life with my mom and my siblings, and back to my old boyfriend. Bryan would check in every so often with a letter or a phone call, nothing serious, just enough to remind me he was there... waiting.

That kind of love, the quiet unhurried kind, was like peace to my restless soul. It soothed and grounded me. That is why it wasn't long before I made my way back to Bryan. We got married at 19 and had 5 kids by the time we were 28. Life became hectic; we were so young and inexperienced. We didn't know how to work together. I think that many marriages are lost here. At first, you can't stand being away from each other; it's glorious and exciting! Then you must learn to live and work together. This transition can cause painful misunderstandings. The stress of making ends meet and running a home are enough to frustrate anyone. But if you remember your intrinsic self and ask God to help you love each other better, God will soon usher you into the most rewarding phase I've found so far. I call it the Co-Creation stage.

I was in my forties before it dawned on me that *I* was responsible for my own happiness! The day I realized that was the day my marriage changed. As soon as I took the death grip off of my husband, he was released to love me on his terms. By the way, his terms are BETTER than anything I could have demanded of him. We started remembering how much we actually liked each other. Bryan has always been there for me in his divine masculine, waiting like he waited when I returned home to my mom back in high school. Waiting for me to embrace my divine feminine so our journey could enter into a new realm of being. The grace he continues to offer me allows our sex life to be a source of healing and bliss for both of us!

With Radical Responsibility came Radical Forgiveness. And the more we forgive each other, the more room we have to receive greater Light and Knowledge! And I KNOW you have access to the same intrinsic knowing that I do!

Let me leave you with an experience I just had while writing this chapter...

Unleashing Creativity

One day as I was writing this chapter for you, I was having a hard time feeling and finding inspiration. The Spirit whispered, "Go take a walk in the park." I said, "Yeah, that's a good idea. But I have to WRITE this chapter! The deadline is near!"

God said, "Haben, come play with me!"

I said, "Okay."

I got ready, got in my car, and drove to my favorite park. As I was figuring out where to go, I saw a trail I'd never walked before and thought, "I'll go there." I had two choices–left or right. Normally, I choose right. But this time, the Spirit whispered, "Try left today," so I did. It felt weird, awkward, and even a little bit wrong to go left. But that's what the Spirit said to do, so that's what I did.

Now I said, "Okay, Heavenly Father, what is it you want me to learn today? Remember I have this chapter that I have to write, and I don't know what I'm going to say...

I REALLY Need Help Right Now! I Need to feel Inspired!"

I walked around a bend in the trail, and the Spirit said, "Look over there." I looked. There I saw one solitary yellow iris next to the pond I was walking by. It was the only one left, the last one from spring. I KNEW that iris was there for me to REMIND me to trust that God loves me and wants me to be successful.

It's because of experiences like this that I Know that He Loves me. But it's not just me He loves. It's ALL of us! It's YOU and me, the women, the men, and of course, the children. He Loves ALL of His children.

Because He knows me and how I love to shine through my gifts and talents, He encourages me to use my voice as a witness to remind you How MUCH He LOVES YOU!

I saw up ahead that part of the path had been beaten up with tire tracks. The earth was exposed. The grass had been worn away. Rain had created a puddle there. Now it was dry, but it was still dirty and torn up from where tires had splashed through and created a muddy puddle. I was given another option: go through the center and get my white tennis shoes dirty and possibly twist my ankle, or go right and walk on what remained of the existing path, which was still smooth. I started walking right, but then I looked over to my left. The path was still bare and bumpy but much less treacherous. It looked like the kind of thing you would want to walk on as a kid. It looked like the earth would make that satisfying crunch noise under your feet. I thought, "I want to take that path." So I did. It was fun. Not in a BIG way. But it *was* fun. I thought, "I just chose left again. See how much FUN it can be to Change!"

Embracing Change and Joy

Our whole lives, we're taught to fear change. Change could mean we have to move and leave all our friends. Change could mean someone we love dying. Or that we lose our job or get divorced. And it's true. Change can mean all of that.

But guess what else change can mean! Change can also mean going down a different path and being led to see a BEAUTIFUL iris. Change can mean choosing a different side of the same path, but just a little more Exciting. Change can mean accepting Radical Trust in God with your life in ways you don't understand yet. But you "know" it... you feel it in your bones. So you reach out, and you ask to be a co-author in an International #1 Best Selling Book.

Boy is that change Scary and Exciting and Fun and LIFE CHANGING in a Good Way!

So my friends, what can you do to allow that kind of Change to happen in your life today? Fun, Happy change.

If change is inevitable, why not just stand up and say to Heavenly Father,

"I'll do it!

But I'd like to do it this way.

Is that okay?

Is it okay for me to ask if I can do it in a fun way, instead of a hard way?

Is it okay for me to ask to learn my lessons quickly, instead of long, drawn-out, and painful?

Is it okay for me to really enjoy my marriage? Can I be married to a man who *cherishes* me and whom I LOVE spending time with? Can we, TOGETHER, create a life full of abundance?

Is it okay if we have nice things, not because I am vain or proud but because I really enjoy BEAUTY, and I love being surrounded by beautiful things because they remind me how much you love me?

Is it okay if my family and I travel all over the world to be reminded that you created this *amazing* world for us to explore?

Can I ask to do it that way?

I'd much rather do it that way."

Heavenly Father looks at me and over at Heavenly Mother and with tears running down both their faces they say,

"Yes, Haben! Yes, of course, you can do it that way.

We've just been waiting for you to ASK.

We've been waiting for you to BELIEVE that's what you can Have.

We have so much to give you.

We have more to give than pain, sorrow, anger, and strife.

We created this world for you to have Joy, but so many of you are focused on the negative. So many of you lose yourselves in the weaknesses you were given. But now that you know that you can ask for all good things and trust that you can learn your lessons in positive ways as well as the painful and hard ways...

Now that you know you can do this in easy and fun ways too; now we can remind you that your weaknesses were designed to stretch and grow you rather than defeat you. Your Strengths far outweigh your weaknesses. Wake up, Daughters! Wake the Wild Woman Within. *REMEMBER* who you ARE! *REMEMBER* that *You* are our Daughter and we love co-creating with you.

So come and play with us!"

Dedicated to my Mom, my husband Bryan, my Creator, and to the Wild Woman within all of us.

ABOUT THE AUTHOR

HABEN DELALLATA

HABEN DELALLATA has been a homeschooling stay-at home mom of five beautiful children who are now between the ages of 15-23. She has been married for 24 year and is passionate about teaching women to appreciate the divine masculine in their husbands so that their marriages can blossom like hers has. She is inspired by all things holistic and has studied herbalism, essential oils and energy healing. She sees God in all things and loves to empower women to find their source so that they can awaken their intention and become co-creators of their lives.

Haben creates sacred experiences, culminating in retreats, for women to unleash their untamed woman within. She does this by guiding them through body movement, sacred sound bathes and bringing them into the rawness of nature, all of which allows them to connect more deeply to the Divine; their higher self; and ultimately return to love.

Connect with Haben here:

Website: https://habendelallata.com/

Freebie: Bath Ritual with a free Bath Bomb recipe. Connect via Facebook to receive this.

Facebook: https://www.facebook.com/haben.travlin.del

SOOCHEN LOW

FROM SERVANT GIRL TO SOVEREIGN QUEEN

*P*our yourself a wine and join me in a heart-to-heart conversation with Marie, one of my former clients.

Marie: Soochen, now that I've gained my sovereignty where I'm now Queen of my Queendom, Queen of my Castle, I feel such amazing power and right to be me. It's so freeing! It's delicious. It feels so yummy and so expansive inside that I sometimes get a bit afraid of how good it feels.

But if I can be really honest, whilst I'm enjoying this freedom to be fully ME, knowing that I'm entitled to be who I am- warts and all; with my shadow now in the light, proud and strong-

It's scary as hell to be in sovereignty!

I've wanted this sovereignty, this entitlement to be me—the right to be me, without apology, for as long as I can remember. This was what I've always dreamt of. I've been busy trying to tick all the boxes—the $10K months, business, clients, money, house, car, marriage, kids, time, place, situations, and circumstances—in the hopes that they would grant me sovereignty. However, after doing the deep work with you, claiming my sovereignty FIRST without needing to check all the boxes has ironically and miraculously allowed them all to flow in, effortlessly and abundantly!

I can't even begin to express how grateful I am to you, the Universe, my guides, and myself for collaborating and bringing this surreal yet beautiful reality come to pass. And yet, with this newfound right and power, it also feels unfamiliar and uncomfortable when I try to take aligned actions from my throne as Queen of my life.

Fact is, this is so new to me. I've spent my entire life waiting for someone else to grant me the right to be myself. I was waiting for that powerful external source to decree or ordain, "Marie, you now have the right to be who you are, exactly in the unique way that you were born and designed to be in this life. Now go forth and be you; it's safe, and it's OK to be you." But I never heard it. I believed that when God was dishing out "Entitlement to be Unique," he ran out of it when he got to me; I was forgotten and had to walk away without it.

Now working with you, I learnt that this right was always something I had to take, to claim for myself because it is *my birthright*.

What a revelation! An eye-opener! A long-overdue relief and years of weight evaporated! A deep satisfaction right to my heart and soul!

Soochen: Oh, Marie, I'm so happy to hear you say this! You've come such a long, long way from when we first met. Similar to me, you're someone who values your freedom of expression; your calling and passion are downloaded from your multidimensional self. I knew there was a predestined reason for us to meet and work together.

Marie: It's so funny that you say that because I felt you spoke to my soul when we first met. I could see and feel you have a nonlinear perspective that transcends our daily challenges, your clarity and wisdom comes from years in the trenches working things out, and your practical roadmap leads to magic and abundance! I felt in my heart you are my North Star to guide me out of being enslaved by the 3D conditions. I'm so glad I followed my intuition because the results and transformation I have enjoyed are beyond anything I have ever experienced.

Soochen: Aww, thank you so much for saying that! It means we both remember our soul contract to help you alchemize your shadow and show you the way to unleash your creative power so you can finally be in control of your income, life, and destiny. I feel you deeply because I know the pain of having a BIG spirit and soul level work but being trapped by the conditions and expectations of life, confused with no way out. This is why I'm so passionate about sharing why it's so important to move away from being the Servant Girl in our lives and businesses and BE the Queen we were born to be.

Marie: So you too were a Servant Girl in your life?

Soochen: Absolutely, I was! I was the firstborn in a traditional Chinese family. As a creative spirit, I was very rebellious and curious; always running around trying new things and testing the boundaries. My parents thought, "Oh my God! If we don't rein this girl in and discipline her, who knows what kinds of trouble she's going to get into." So out of their most loving intentions to protect this little powerhouse who was new to the ways of the material world, they put in place rules, conditions, and expectations as their means of setting boundaries to protect me.

As a result, I grew up learning that I needed to tick boxes and meet expectations. To be smart, I needed to get good grades. To be responsible, I needed to complete my chores. To be respectful, I had to remain silent when the adults spoke. To be praised for being a good and tidy girl, I had to never make a mess when eating at the table. I quickly realized that when I'm a good girl, Mom and Dad are pleased with me. I am loved when I do the right thing. I was severely punished if I did not. Bad things happen to you when you don't fulfill conditions and meet up expectations. It wasn't until my sister came along about four and a half years later that I witnessed a change in my Mum and Dad.

I saw the rules that applied to me did not apply to her. They shaped and worked around her in ways they never did for me.

What I took away from that tender age was I needed to be my sister to be safe, loved, and accepted. If I was me, then I wasn't. In hindsight, when I looked back on why my parents did not apply the same rules I had to my sister, it was because she was a quiet and serene soul, utterly different from me, and naturally did not require the exact boundaries as I did. In fact, she was content to follow me around, and with me as her role model, my parents realized that she required a different set of parameters from me.

Without the beauty of hindsight or maturity to help me out then, I started feeling jealous, constantly comparing myself to my sister, wishing I was her. Because if I were, then I wouldn't need to fulfill expectations and meet up with the rules and conditions. I could just be me—rebellious, curious, naughty, plus all my other quirks. And even if I didn't tick a particular box, I would still be loved and safe. Deep in my heart, my wish of wishes was to be my sister because she represented to me what it looked like to have the right to be unique.

As I was not her, I thought the only option I had was to earn my place by working harder as the servant girl to my family, teachers, friends, and later in life, husband, clients, business, time, money, situations, and circumstances. I was constantly bound by the power over, power under dynamic, where I was always on my knees looking up to that external force, believing that was the only way for me to be rewarded in dollars, love, time, approval, and worthiness in exchange for the hours, conditions and expectations I worked to fulfill. It was the constant, never-ending transactional nature of "If I do this, then I get that" to earn my worth, my place, and my lovability as a woman and leader of my life and businesses-

If I work hard and slave to death, I get the money.

If I do this for you, then I get your love and approval.

If I make you happy, then I am safe.

If I make $10K months, then I am successful and worthy.

The list went on and on. The more I pushed and chased to tick the endless boxes, the more I kept myself down on my knees instead of on my throne as Sovereign Queen.

Marie: Oh my goodness! How on earth did you manage to find your creative power from such a deep-rooted place?

Soochen: Yes, outwardly, you would never guess I suffered from feeling less because I looked 'successful' and came across as very confident. Ironically, I had built up an inflated and false sense of self, deriving a great sense of satisfaction and achievement, thinking I was doing all the 'right' things and being praised by others for them. But my envy, jealousy, resentment, and anger towards my sister could not be suppressed any longer. And eventually, it exploded into destructive behaviors where I sabotaged her and our family business. I was even asked to leave as I had become very toxic by then and clearly expressed through my attitude and actions that I no longer wanted to be a part of the family and business.

So there I was, alone and with only $200 in my bank account. I was incredibly ashamed, shell-shocked that I was capable of creating such chaos when I had spent my whole life doing all the 'right' things, thinking I was 'all that'. In my moments of weakness trying to take the 'easy' way out, I contemplated ending my life many times, but the idea that things could turn out far worse if I didn't do it right stopped me. The only other option was to clean up my life and make a change. The thought did cross my mind, "Who are you to think you can clean it up and change when all around you is the crap you created?" For the sake of self-preservation and the glimmer of hope that my life could not possibly end there—I crawled, stumbled, and took one baby step at a time, fumbling in the dark, looking for *my* light at the end of the tunnel.

And that was when and how my Happy.Positive.Successful Formula was born; you know it now as the Monetize your Creative Power method that we worked through together.

What I discovered was that my full creative power was hidden in the embarrassing 'shit' I had been taught to hide, or what I now refer to as your 'shadow.' They were the things about me that I'd learnt over time as "too emotional, too sensitive, too selfish, too weak, too strong," etc., that I was too embarrassed to own up to and had hidden at the back of the closet and swept under the rug. When I went through my healing process of bringing everything from my shadow into the light with the intention to see and extract only the potential and transmute them into wisdom and power, I began to tap into the other 95% of my full creative power. And that was when things started to shift and change for the better.

Marie: Yes, when I first learnt of your method, I was skeptical it could work for me too. But true to the Creative Power Business Alchemist in you, this is definitely your magic where you unearthed my crap, radically accepted it, extracted the potential that I never knew existed, and transmuted it into literal gold in dollars, wisdom, and power! Every time I see the powerful woman I have become and the wealthy, abundant lifestyle I now enjoy, I'm so proud of myself! But Soochen, did you do all this on your own, or did you have external help?

Soochen: Hmm, people often ask me this. I was so ashamed of the crap and chaos I created. To contain the damage, I quarantined and isolated myself to do the deep inner work so I wouldn't spread it to more people before I was completely healed. At the time, I thought I shut down my clairaudient connection to my immortal family in the multi-D, not trusting my guidance. In hindsight, of course, we are never alone, and this seemingly awful and debilitating experience was the most beautiful, Divine, and powerful catalyst to awaken the Sovereign Queen in me. Happily, I am now reconciled with my sister and family and have come to a deeper level of understanding and respect for each other. This work is so close to my heart because when I was all 'alone' in my rock bottom days, I had 'no one' to turn to, and so I've made it my life's work to be that support for others who may be going through similar journeys.

I've learned that being yourself and understanding your right not to be trapped by or meet the conditions of others is the first step toward becoming less of a servant girl and more of a Sovereign Queen. You have the absolute right to have whatever you want, WITHOUT any trade, exchange, or transaction. Make your claim without having to prove, explain, defend, or justify it. It just is, and so it is.

Marie: Soochen, I love this, and I'm so glad to hear you are reunited with your family! But I've often wondered if claiming what I want makes me selfish?

Soochen: It's understandable and very common. When I first came into my sovereignty, the entitlement and power came with an amplified clarity that I was also being the Servant Girl in my marriage in a plethora of ways— fulfilling conditions and expectations that I thought would allow me to be loved, accepted, treasured, protected, and nurtured. I'm grateful to my husband for being the catalyst and teacher to help me see that our relationship was based on who I was when we first met- the Servant Girl and when I claimed my sovereignty, it was evident we were no longer in alignment.

When I needed to make the tough decision to hold on or let go of the relationship, I too, asked myself if I was being selfish by putting myself first. Contemplating whether I was being selfish or if it was better to be selfless made me more conflicted. So I wondered, "To cling on means I would need to continue to suffocate myself, dim my passion, silence my voice, suppress my desires, and turn my back on my soul purpose- is this in integrity to me, to the other person and for humanity?"

My answer was No. If I were to continue to be the Servant Girl, I would be teaching others by example that they are justified to demand that I fulfill their conditions and expectations. In turn, I would be condoning others in their lives to do the same to them. By honoring and allowing me to put myself first, I was, in fact, honoring their right to stop being servants to the people in their lives. As a ripple effect, we can then all be leaders of our own lives and our businesses and be the inspiration for those around us to each stand in our sovereignty and claim our right to be uniquely us.

Marie: Wow, your answer hits me right in my heart, but I don't think I could handle it if everybody turned away from me for choosing to honor me.

Soochen: Oh, I know what you mean! The idea of letting go of what I thought was a very loving relationship was excruciating. Our greatest fear is that when we honor who we uniquely are, others will judge us and not love us anymore. As someone who used to exist and thrived on others' good opinions of me and died a little inside when they didn't, I know this fear so well.

However, in the spirit of love, I decided to shine the light on how **I** was feeling inside for a change- the frustration, resentment, anger of always being silenced, and the heart-wrenching pain when I silenced myself of my own volition because I was afraid I would lose their love. I'd learnt that true love is unconditional, and I will not accept anything less. So if being ME is failing someone else's condition, then it mustn't be true love and needs to be let go of to honor me. Those who truly love me unconditionally will remain and celebrate my sovereignty. Whilst those who don't will move on and make space for truly loving relationships to flow into my life.

Marie: Oh! Your answer fills me with such peace. Thank you! You know, I feel more empowered now about exercising my right and power as Sovereign Queen.

But I'm still afraid that I would somehow abuse my power and lose myself.

Soochen: I, like you, when I first stepped into my sovereignty, was, " Wow! I've never had this before! This power, this sense of freedom, this weightlessness, you almost feel quite heady that it's a bit scary. It feels so euphoric that you wonder if you are now drunk with power and intoxicated by your right that maybe you will become 'entitled' and start to be destructive, hurtful, insensitive, mean, aggressive, and abusive to others.

Marie: That's exactly how I feel!

Soochen: Yes, when I went inward and reflected more on this, I realized I was lumping myself in with the manipulative and spoiled brat Queen image. This made sense to some degree because I, too, had been destructive, manipulative, and hurtful to others in my life. I now know that the person I was back then came from a place of lack where I did not feel I had the right to be uniquely me. So in a fit of rebellion or defiance, I acted out negatively. Upon realization in my healing process, there was a lot of myself in the shadow, instead of allowing it to continue to trip me up unconsciously or subconsciously at every turn moving forward. I did the challenging inner work to extract authenticity, integrity, and alignment to Divine purpose instead of chasing superficial power. As a result, the Sovereign Queen in me was unleashed. Through this process, I found myself, came to own and harness my authentic creative power trusting that whenever I unleash it, being of service will always be my intuitive compass where I do not ever need to fear I would abuse my well-earned sovereignty.

Marie: That's SO inspiring! I'm looking forward to continuing my process with you so I, too, can wield my power for my highest good and humanity, trusting that my expansion and growth are always aligned to my purpose!

Soochen: And so it is!

ABOUT THE AUTHOR

SOOCHEN LOW

SOOCHEN LOW is a Creative Power Alchemist, Founder of Happy.Positive.Successful, International #1 Bestselling Author and International Keynote Speaker.

With 30 years experience in the coaching, hospitality and haircare industry, she helps female creative coaches and entrepreneurs grow their businesses to consistent $10K months without struggle, people-pleasing, or having to prove themselves. She does this by harnessing their creativity to build supportive business structures, customized to their genius, so they can own their unique power and be in control of their income, life and destiny.

Soochen holds a BDesign with First Class Honours in Fashion Design and MBA from University of Technology in Management & Managing for Sustainability. An inspiring speaker, she has changed the lives of millions of listeners on the Chinese online platform CC Talk with her Monetize your Creative Power methodology and is a regular guest on summits and podcasts.

Young at heart, body, mind and spirit, Soochen *loves* people, is a *stand* for their sovereignty and a testament of the magic and abundance that flows into your life when you own, harness and unleash your unique creative power.

Connect with Soochen:

Website: www.happypositivesuccessful.com

Free Masterclass Video: Grow your biz to $10K months: https://bit.ly/3aOmEcU

FREE Monetize your Creative Power Strategy call: https://ed.gr/durs8

PART IV

IGNITING JOY

DR. ANTON GILLEZEAU

THE EXPLORATION OF CONSCIOUSNESS AND THE JOURNEY TO EXPERIENCING MORE JOY IN LIFE

*L*et's dance and smile as if no one's watching, and if they are, simply smile back.

As I contemplated writing this chapter and put my fingers on the keyboard, a simple and somewhat obvious question struck me.

What exactly does it mean to live an inspired life?

What do we consider joy to be, what does it look like and feel like, and do we always recognise it when we experience it?

This question makes me smile as it brought up for me the phenomenon that we can be so busy doing life, achieving things first by ticking off the to-do list with all the 'shoulds' before allowing ourselves the simple pleasure of experiencing joy at the moment.

We can be so busy attending to the everyday stuff of life that by the time we're done, we've lost our inspiration because we're too drained or have run out of time to do more creative activities, and they get put off to the next day. The danger is that the next day can inexorably become 'one day' and that that day never comes.

The different flavours of joy and how we experience them

There have been treatises written on this question ranging from philosophical to psychological and ultimately spiritual perspectives, and we will all have our own perspectives on how this manifests in our own life.

It may be different for you, but whenever I tap into the feeling of joy or acknowledge it in the moment, it seems such an innocent, simple, and pure feeling. Feeling joyous doesn't really need a reason.

There are many other expanded or uplifting states that we recognise as positive.

Feeling happy is the closest to joy and the most obvious one. We can also feel a sense of achievement, fulfilment, or being proud of something we've done or someone we love as just a few of the many things that bring us joy and happiness.

There are states of excitement that come from all sorts of activities such as skiing down a mountain, attending a concert, spending time in nature or quality time with friends, and if it's with the right person, sex.

Joy feels more like an allowing. A letting go of all the mind chatter, the mental constructs around what's meant to make us feel good or bring us happiness, and simply allowing yourself to BE in the moment. Children often embody this state naturally; for us adults, it seems to be much more of a challenge.

Why not ask yourself this question and see what comes up for you? Give it a moment and don't think too hard; just allow. As I ask this of myself, I connect to the feeling states they evoke and try to discern if there's a difference. They are very closely aligned, but there does seem to be a subtly different flavour to each one.

I tend to associate happiness with being more dynamic somehow. If life feels good, we can have that feeling of just being happy, light, and energised as an overall state as we go through our day. It seems though that we often feel happy because something external has ignited that in us. Those things can be unique to each of us, depending on our personalities and values.

One person's party can be another's idea of hell.

When I drop in and tune into joy, the sensation is spacious, expansive, yet somehow calming. It doesn't feel like there needs to be a reason as such, and it can come to us quite spontaneously, too, at times.

If you ask me to cut to the chase and give you the fastest way to consciously inspire joy from the inside out, then feeling gratitude is the key.

Regardless of my current circumstance, mood, or external stresses, I make a habit every day over breakfast to write down at least three things I am grateful for both in this moment and why. They can be from the past, present, and also from a desired future, as if that future has already unfolded in the way you truly want.

As I feel the essence of gratitude and love for all that is washing over me, I experience a calmness, openness, and stillness from which joy emerges. Feeling joyful doesn't need an object, person, or external experience to elicit it. It seems as much a tranquil or being state as opposed to an excited or doing state.

Memories of Joy

As an exercise, I went back over my life from early childhood and sifted through the memories to find the activities, moments, and experiences that brought me joy. Our childhood can leave clues as children don't tend to overthink life to the extent we learn to do as we get older. If they like something, they do it, and if they're told "No," they often find a way to do it anyway.

If I think about my early childhood memories, I remember I felt most joyous when I was playing on my own. I was an only child until age seven when my brother was born, so I had a lot of time to be on my own. What came to me was the sense of being utterly present with the activities I loved to do, such as Lego, reading and drawing, somewhat badly, I'm happy to admit. Playing with matchbox cars and later building Airfix model planes with all the fabric of my childhood imagination woven in to bring those activities to life.

At that age, I was also fascinated by astronomy. As it happened, the space race was well and truly on as Man geared up to go to the moon, so it was very much in the zeitgeist. My parents being teachers and valuing the pursuit of enquiry and knowledge, supported this interest. I was even inspired to create a little project book in which I wrote about all the famous astronomers through the ages and what their contributions were.

However, it was contemplating the concept of infinity that I could feel. Not only was my mind stretched, but so was my consciousness, as I imagined counting, then counting some more, then realising there was no end to the counting. I imagined space stretching on until you thought you'd reached the edge only to have it keep on going, at which point my six-year-old mind would pop, and I'd go back to playing with my matchbox cars.

Years later, I would revisit this exploration and expansion while doing Dr. Joe Dispenza's meditations. Especially the ones that specifically invite you to imagine the vastness and energy of space stretching out in every direction around you until you ultimately dissolve into the Oneness and a true state of bliss.

I can now see that there was a spiritual element to all these ponderings, as they begged the question of where all this magnitude and wonder comes from and how extraordinary it is that we have the capacity to contemplate it.

And to be in that wonderment was—and still is—a source of joy for me.

Living in the Box

Having a keen interest in health and wellness, I became a chiropractor, got married, had two children, and provided for my family. I did what I thought was expected of me, and life was good; I was happy... Looking back, I was living in the box of society's expectations and hadn't tapped into the bigger mission of why I am here.

My mission in the world is to keep exploring and expanding both my own and our society's consciousness on all levels. And that includes releasing the complexities of life we have created and returning back to the simplicity of joy and gratitude. I am passionate about helping create a world where individuals have more compassion for each other, understand one another as best we can, and are tolerant of another person's point of view, especially when it differs from our own.

I didn't come to that overnight though.

Wake up, son; you're getting a Divorce

There's nothing like a major unexpected turn of events to make you reassess what's important, what you value, and what you need to let go of in order to move forward.

I never imagined it would happen to me as I was fully committed to my family and marriage. As I gradually accepted and became accustomed to being single after over 20 years of an essentially happy marriage and two beautiful children, I needed ways to find new meaning outside of my role as a husband, father, and provider. All the work of building that life, the incentive to build a thriving chiropractic practice and fulfil my societal and familial obligations, which I had embraced with pleasure, felt very challenging.

I had lost my mojo!

I have always been a very glass-half-full, upbeat, and optimistic person, so having my 22-year marriage end was very confronting.

Needless to say, this wasn't the most joyous period in my life. At the beginning of 2009, we formally separated and rented out the family home. I downsized my dream practice in Avalon on Sydney's Northern Beaches and left to go and live with my father, who then passed away soon after. All this in the space of three months...fun times.

Going on a Quest and Looking in the Mirror

Having done many years of personal development, I was not shy about looking in the mirror and asking myself what part I played in all this dynamic. It is important to go through the process of deconstructing and analysing 'what went wrong' and then ask for the lessons, but it isn't easy. Good thing I had loving friends and family to support me emotionally, for which I am most grateful.

But there comes a point when we can only gain so much by endlessly talking it out or from using our intellectual faculties to come to terms with the sadness, grief, and shock of such a shift in life.

INITIATIONS:

5 Rhythms: Releasing the Pain

The pathway to finding more joy and inspiration for life came somewhat out of the left-field, as these things often do. I remember clearly being at a friend's Sunday afternoon soiree at a large top-story apartment in Redfern, Sydney. The sun was shining, and we were enjoying diverse and interesting conversations lounging on its large wrap-around balcony with views of the city skyline.

I got chatting to a particularly entrancing woman who said she'd just come from a 5-rhythms dance class. As she described this free-flowing form of dance meditation, I thought, I've got to try this. So two weeks later, I walked into a large studio on a Sunday morning to find around 70 people preparing for two hours of loosely guided dance.

5 rhythms was developed by Gabriel Roth in New York, and its purpose is to allow us to move through different states as the style of music flows from one form to another. It is an opportunity to use whatever feelings, emotions, and issues we are sitting with and transmute them through the movement of our bodies with total freedom of expression.

Only thirty minutes into my first class, my face began to melt into a smile I couldn't wipe off. As I experimented with moving my body to the music, it struck me that I could dance any way that I wanted. There were no steps or rules as such; it was about literally letting my body interpret the music and follow the feeling of how and where I felt compelled to go.

I danced like no one was watching because nobody really was and felt a sense of liberation that filled me with joy...

5 rhythms unlocked those stuck emotions and allowed them to flow and be released. I went to 5 rhythms religiously for the next ten years. It was a huge part of my journey into connecting with my feelings, allowing myself to feel sadness or grief if that's what was there, as well as the thrilling exhilaration of simply enjoying what my body could do. Surprising myself by testing my edges and always coming away feeling a complete change of state no matter how I was upon arrival.

There are traditions in every culture of us, human beings, being transported by dance and music; however, it is easy to neglect this oldest of creative expression in the humdrum of everyday busy lives unless we seek it out.

I realised that we can't just think our way through to healing, change, and transformation, we have to embody it somehow, and dance was, for me at least, a powerful part of my journey back to more joy and appreciation of life.

Tantra: Life Force Energy Revived

At the same time as I discovered 5 rhythms dance, I was also introduced to Tantra. Having found myself single for the first time since the age of 22, this was an opportunity to connect with women in a safe and respectful environment; it opened the door to exploring the masculine and feminine essences within that are part of us all, whether we are consciously aware of that or not.

However, there were clearly much more subtle reasons that my ex had been trying to communicate to me that I just didn't quite get. Delving into tantra allowed me to explore the subtle and sometimes not so subtle energies that arise. Most of the evenings at that time were relatively tame in terms of the exercises, but it allowed me to connect to a different level of awareness when it came to how or why a woman would respond to me or not, as the case may be.

There were times to be open and vulnerable, times to be forthright and strong, lead or be lead, feel sexy or more nurturing, safe or edgier. Being an embodied practice, tantra has allowed me to become much more sensitive to the energetic cues in both men and women and in myself.

It was another piece in the journey of coming back to more joy by allowing myself to be more fully me, well, outside of the identities and expectations of professional or family life, and to enjoy that without judgement.

Judgement, whether of oneself or of others, does anything but bring joy.

In all these practices the acceptance and releasing of sadness, guilt, shame, even anger, and disappointment have paved the way for a lighter, fuller life. Life is about feeling all that here is to feel, then turning towards the expansiveness that awaits that release.

Plant Medicine: Deepening into Gratitude and Love

The final experience that I want to share here is one that took me through a series of epic and sometimes torturous journeys until I could fully embody the two greatest pillars of all spiritual teachings: gratitude and love.

If there has been one thing I've done that taught me about feeling gratitude and love in every cell in my body, often hauling me over the proverbial coals until I really, really felt them, not just said them, it's my journey with plant medicines.

Let me say right off the top, they are definitely not for anyone and everyone unless you feel a calling to experience them.

I got that call while watching a documentary on Netflix one night back in 2016 called DMT, the spirit molecule. I'd read the book as it happens, which is what drew me to it. As I sat there on my own enjoying this well-crafted doco, I experienced something I'd never experienced either before or since.

A momentary sensation of awareness above my head and then a voice, distinct and clear, inside yet outside my head. It said in reference to the documentary I was watching, "See that, that's the next evolution of your consciousness". Even though I knew I was alone it was so clear that I literally took a look around the room for a moment to check as I paused the film.

I didn't think anything more about it until about two weeks later, on a Sunday night, a text message came through on my phone around 9 pm. It was from someone I used to work with but hadn't had any contact with for a year. They suggested there was a retreat they thought I would like in a part of Australia that is the least likely place to have a retreat centre.

Surprised and puzzled, I replied somewhat dubiously, only to have them press a little harder as to how much I might like it, and then out of the blue, the penny dropped, and intuitively, I knew.

They were messaging in response to that mysterious voice.

I went to that retreat and many more. The expansion of consciousness for me was essentially around people and relationships. Lesson one was being clear on my role as warrior-protector to my son and daughter, then rippling out to their mother and on through every member of my family in ever-widening circles to our communities. And ultimately, the planet.

As I focused on each person, the message always came back to fully appreciating them, then truly feeling more gratitude and love. If I didn't feel it deep in my heart and every cell in my body, then the message just got louder until I did.

I would ask about business and get the same message: Just go deeper into gratitude and love, and you will provide more and better service for which you will be rewarded. Information on how better to do things professionally or in business is available by the truckload. However all that success will count for very little if you don't embrace this fundamental principle.

The energy lifted as the journey continued, and by the end, with music and song, it became a true celebration of life in all its wonders. At the end of the night, there was a profound sense of calm, cleansing, and healing that opened the space for more joy and appreciation of all that we get to experience in our lifetime here on this unique planet.

The Return Home

Do you need to have these particular experiences to connect or feel more joy in your life?

Absolutely not; we all have our own journeys.

You can start right now, quietly, while no one's watching. Allow a little smile to play across your lips, shift a little in your chair, and wiggle those hips. And before you know it, the Universe will be joining you in your dance.

ABOUT THE AUTHOR

DR. ANTON GILLEZEAU

DR. ANTON has enjoyed a 35-year career as a Chiropractor both in Sydney and London, focusing on optimising people's potential through natural health and wellness.

He has a passion for bringing people back to the basics of their health and connection to their bodies. Bringing awareness to the quality of their diet and water, exercise, and their psychological and emotional wellbeing.

Anton holds a B.Sc from the University of New South Wales and a Post Grad diploma in Chiropractic with expertise in Kinesiology and Neuro Emotional Technique.

Throughout the last three decades, he has explored the world of personal and spiritual development with mentors such as Dr. John DeMartini, Tony Robbins, and Dr. Joe Dispenza. He has qualifications in NLP and coaching, helping budding entrepreneurs, and facilitating Men's Circles to encourage men to feel heard and safe to express the challenges they face, particularly around relationships.

His mission is to keep exploring and expanding both his own and our society's consciousness on all levels, returning back to the simplicity of expressing joy, love, and gratitude, helping to create a world where we all have more compassion and tolerance for each other and another person's point of view, especially when it is not our own.

Anton currently practices in Sydney, Australia.

Connect with Anton here: https://linktr.ee/dr_anton_gillezeau

EMMA GRAY

LIVING FROM THE INSIDE OUT

Embodied Wisdom

Decoding your body signals to unlock the secrets to inner joy

*M*y little dog Rosie spends most of her day resting. She is lying next to me as I write this. When restless, she will get up and stretch, wander off into the garden, and find things to sniff or roll in the grass. There is a gentle rhythm to her day—rest, activity, rest, activity, rest. Animals have an instinctive knowing, an inner compass that guides them, letting them know when it is time for action and time for rest. This is called Ultradian rhythms, similar to Circadian rhythms (our wake/sleep cycle), but is an activity/rest cycle during the day. As humans, we are physiologically hardwired to require periods of rest and activity.

However, in our modern industrialised world, we have lost touch with the natural rhythms of our bodies. We are pushed to go, go, go all day. More often than not, we are driven by the clock and external pressures. By the demands of our bosses and bank managers, the influence of our friends and family. How would it be if we said to our boss or our kids, "I just need an hour's break, see you later"?

We live from the *Outside In*.

Being the Good Girl

When my brother was ten years old, he was diagnosed with a brain tumour. I was eight at that time. This was a period of incredible stress for my parents, and their attention was understandably taken up with his needs. As an empath, I absorbed the distress in the family. I was a very anxious child, and it was scary for me to see others in distress, so I tried to help in whatever way I could. I took it upon myself to look after my little sister, to take the load off my parents. I played with her and read her stories. She snuggled up with me in bed at night if she was scared or lonely. I suppose my little mind thought that if everyone else were okay, then I would be okay. My role became being a Soother and a Helper. I was the Good Girl. Looking back, I realise that I ignored my own needs to ease the pressure on the family. I made myself invisible; I developed patterns of self-sacrifice and people-pleasing. It was my way of coping to avoid anxiety and discomfort. I was trying to make myself safe by disappearing. All my focus was on other people and their needs, so I became oblivious to what I needed or wanted. I was living from the *Outside In*.

While this was a difficult time, I can also see that it was early training for my Calling. I became really good at reading people, at sensing their emotions and what they need. I am often told that I have a very calming energy and a soothing voice. It's not surprising that I ended up working as a psychologist, coach, and meditation teacher. I help others find ways to reduce stress and cultivate calm. I have been doing this since I was that eight-year-old girl.

Finding your Ikigai

I love helping people. It brings me deep joy to help others thrive, to help them discover what makes them happy. When I was in my early twenties, I remember I would go to parties, meet people and ask them, "What do you do?" and then ask, "Do you enjoy that?". If they didn't, I'd find myself wanting to coach them (before I even knew what coaching was). I wanted to help them find something that made them happy. In Japan, there is a concept called *Ikigai*, which means "reason for being." There is a belief that we are all born with our own unique Ikigai, a sense of purpose. Every soul has a calling. Every soul has a mission or purpose. Every soul is born into this lifetime with a powerful intention. And figuring that out is a part of our journey in this lifetime. To hear the Call of our Soul. To figure out what our mission is. To listen to our Inner Compass and live from the *Inside Out.*

Our sense of deepest fulfilment comes from living our Ikigai, utilising our natural strengths. Doing the things that feel natural, that feel easy, that feel fun and effortless. That, for others, may seem challenging or complicated— but for us, it just comes naturally—the place that feels like home. My Ikigai is to help others find peace and joy, thrive and live their *calling*, and live their most Inspired Lives.

I had no idea about any of this as a young woman venturing out in life. I was utterly disconnected from my own inner guidance while working in the corporate world. I had no interest in business strategy, and the bottom line: I was totally in the wrong job. (And I'm sure my bosses thought so, too!). I craved something more meaningful. I wanted to help people get happy. But how could I help other people get happy if I didn't know how to do that for myself?

I left the corporate world to have babies and study psychology (which was my first step to listening to my Inner Compass), but still, it felt like my life was unravelling. The Universe had a powerful message for me, and I wasn't listening yet. I was still living from the *Outside In.* I was still a self-sacrificing, people-pleaser, in an unhealthy relationship, and did not look after myself. Both of my babies had colic. They cried a lot. I was sleep-deprived and exhausted. The only time-out I had was for dental appointments. Things are not great if your special me-time is a visit to the dentist! I spent my time cleaning up baby puke and watching the Wiggles. I felt lonely, anxious, burnt out, and unfulfilled. I didn't know who I was or what made me happy.

As my life unravelled, I became fascinated by people who had found peace amid suffering. My intuition urged me to learn as much as I could. I loved the Dalai Lama and Ekhart Tolle. I devoured books by Neale Donald Walsh, Martha, Beck, Byron Katie, Louise Hay, and Esther Hicks. I admired Viktor Frankl, Nelson Mandela, Oprah Winfrey, and Ghandi. My bookshelves began to be filled with spiritual teachers living a life of peace and joy, those who overcame adversity and made a meaningful difference in the world. I wanted to know the secrets to happiness, to living a meaningful life. I read, listened, watched, and absorbed as much as I could. I tried lots of different things because I wanted to know the secrets to inner happiness.

Finding Inner Joy

Then I discovered meditation. It wasn't easy at first. My mind was restless, and I found it challenging to sit for more than 5 minutes! But my inner guidance compelled me to keep going. Each time I practised; it got a little easier. I settled deeper in the silence. My body revelled in the opportunity to rest. My mind started to unwind. I began to feel a gentle yet profound sense of peace. And I noticed something weird start to happen. My body began buzzing; it felt like a humming or vibrating sensation. It became so pronounced that my head gently and rhythmically nodded. It must have looked very odd, but it felt pleasant. Awesome, in fact. I could feel electric energy flowing through my body. I didn't know what it was, but I enjoyed it! I didn't realise, at the time, that this was my body in powerful connection with Source energy. And it still happens to this day when I meditate deeply. It's a gentle buzzing, vibrating humming in my body. A feeling of total fulfilment and bliss. Everything else falls away. And I know I don't need anything outside me to be happy. That happiness comes from the *Inside Out*.

So the journey has been coming back to me. Coming into myself. Starting with looking after my physical needs because I was so depleted and burnt out. Gentle and deeply restorative practices like yoga and meditation. I learnt to look after my emotional needs by connecting with people who were supportive of me. I learnt how to listen to my body, knowing that my body signals (emotions and energy levels) are an indicator of where I'm at and what I need. Listening to this Inner Compass helped me find inner joy.

Tuning into our Inner Compass

So how do we tune in to our Inner Compass? How do we discover the things that bring us joy and purpose? Our body is "talking" to us every moment of the day. It sends subtle (and not so subtle) signals that will light up a clear path to everything we want in life when we listen to them. A path to joy, love, prosperity, and miracles. You can learn to decode these signals and harness the power of your body/spirit connection to live the amazing life that your soul is calling you towards.

Decoding the Signals

I invite you to try a simple exercise to listen to your body. Pause for a moment, close your eyes, and focus on your body. How does it feel right now?

Is it tired, restless, hungry, or relaxed? Notice energy levels, emotions, and sensations.

Now bring to mind a task that you don't like doing, something stressful or uncomfortable. *What happens in your body? What emotions come up? What sensations do you feel?*

You may notice:

Tension, anxiety, stress, overwhelm, aversion, fatigue, heaviness, etc.

This is the body wisdom saying 'NO.'

Now imagine doing something relaxing or fun. *What happens in your body? What emotions come up? What sensations do you feel?*

You may notice:

Ease, relief, lightness, openness, relaxation, warmth, joy, energy, alertness, etc.

This is the body wisdom saying 'YES,' do more of this.

Your body reacts every moment of the day with every thought, activity, and interaction. I invite you to get curious and start to bring mindful awareness to your body responses to your daily life. You will notice the things that energise and uplift you; and those that drain you. You are being guided by your Inner Compass. You are being shown clues that will light up your path to your ideal life.

Ultradian Rhythms

Perhaps, we can learn from animals like my dog Rosie, following her instincts for activity and rest throughout the day (following her ultradian rhythms). Just like the animals of our planet, our bodies need lots of time out during the day. Ideally, for every 90 minutes of activity, we need about 20 minutes of rest. If we don't rest, we start to feel fatigued. If we continue to push ourselves, our minds and body get tired. We may feel irritable, stressed, and eventually burnt out. However, if we have rest breaks throughout the day, we become more productive and energised. We also feel happier and a lot less irritable!

Getting into Ultradian flow

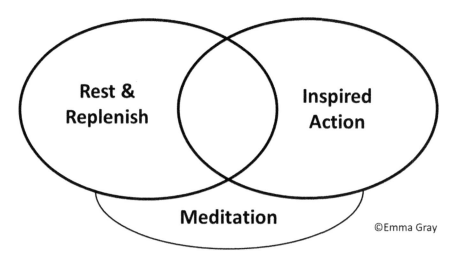

©Emma Gray

Embodied wisdom helps us optimise energy, creativity, joy, performance, and wellbeing.

Take a moment to consider your daily rhythms. Are your rest/activity cycles out of balance? Contemplate the following questions to tune into your ultradian rhythms and Body Wisdom. There are two powerful modes of Being which can transform our lives and lead us to joy and miracles:

Miracle Mode #1: Rest & Replenish

Do I need more time out for myself? What deeply replenishes me mentally, emotionally, physically, and spiritually? How could I incorporate more of this into my daily life?

As you identify things that replenish you, you might make them part of your daily routine. E.g.

Morning routine

- Breakfast
- 15minute meditation or walk
- 1-minute gratitude practice

Bedtime routine

- Warm bath
- 5 minutes of gentle stretching

- Read a book or listen to a relaxing guided meditation

If you are trying to manage a family or a high-pressure job or any other endless responsibilities you may have, this can seem too much. I get it. When my kids were little, and I was juggling work and study, routines like this would have felt impossible. Maybe you could start small, e.g., take 5 or 10 deep breaths before getting out of bed or take a 5-minute walk. It may feel like just one more thing to add to your "to-do" list, but it doesn't have to be a big thing to make a difference. As your body recharges, you will notice a shift in your energy. And if you keep at it, over time, you will cultivate more joy and vitality, and the people around you will start to notice.

Miracle Mode #2: Inspired Action

"Follow your Bliss, and the Universe will open doors where before there were only walls."

Joseph Campbell

What are my interests & passions? What is fun or enjoyable for me? What brings me a sense of meaning and purpose? How could I do more of this?

Taking inspired action is the fun part. Doing things that bring you a sense of joy or meaning. It could be simple things, like spending time with pets or loved ones, spending time in nature, or engaging in fun adventures or creative pursuits. Psychologist Mihaly Csikszentmihalyi identified what he called the "flow" state, where we are so engaged in the moment that we lose track of time. Meditation is a potent tool to gain clarity on what inspires us. Meditation quiets the mind and cultivates connection with the Higher Self. This is the source of inspiration. And that voice can be heard in stillness.

Inspired action can lead us to a Higher Calling. One of my favourite quotes is from the author Jean Houston, who says, *"the Soul is the lure of our becoming."* Every soul is born into this lifetime with a powerful intention, with desires about who and what they want to be. In the words of Oprah Winfrey, *"Everybody has a calling, and your real job in life is to figure out what that is and get about the business of doing it."*

As I followed my Inner Guidance (immersing myself in meditation, mindfulness, yoga, and eastern approaches to wellbeing), alongside other things which felt good, it all led me to my dream job. Every day I get to use my passions in my "work." Mindfulness, meditation, psychology, coaching, and helping people discover their path to their true Calling. My work feels like home. Like this is exactly where I am meant to be. Every time I sit with a client, I feel intensely alive. I feel joyful. I could leap in the air; I feel so happy! In fact, sometimes I actually do jump up in the air when a client has a breakthrough or a big win. I feel so happy for them that I literally jump for joy! (Yes, I know I'm a bit weird!). And as much as possible, I try to be like Rosie. I try to listen to my body and those ultradian rhythms, taking lots of rest breaks when needed. As I do that, I have more creative energy to pursue the things which bring me great joy.

When we identify who we are and what our Soul wants to express in this lifetime, life can be richer, meaningful, and rewarding. Things start to unfold with ease and flow. Opportunities arise that you never dreamed possible. Life becomes more fun and joyful. Synchronicities abound. Life takes on an almost magical quality.

Do you have a sense that life is calling you to something more? A sense that you have a Higher Purpose? Do you feel you were meant for something deeper and greater?

And how do you discover your Calling? How do you know what your soul is calling you towards? Our Soul speaks to us in whispers, gently guiding us and lighting up our path. If we get quiet and listen to our intuition and our body's signals, it will show us that path forward. A compelling starting point is to meditate. As we meditate, we quiet our mind, and our vibration rises. This creates space for inspiration to flow. We get a flow of *ideas* that feel good. We get the urge to *take action* that feels good.

The body signals that indicate we are on the path to everything we want are the emotions and sensations in the body that *feel good.*

Body signals for inspired action:

Joy, enthusiasm, elation, excitement, alertness, increased energy and motivation, urge to take action

This is the Body Wisdom saying "YES," do this!

Living from the Inside Out

My brother survived his brain tumour at age 10. The doctors told my parents that he would probably only live until the age of 20. But he lived until he was 34. He packed a lot of living in those 34 years. He lived from the *Inside Out.*

He had an adventurous spirit. He took risks, often coming home with cuts and scrapes and, sometimes, broken bones (much to the consternation of my mother!). But he wasn't afraid to live life fully. He had adventures; he skydived, rode motorbikes, took dance classes, met the love of his life, and had a baby boy before he passed away. He lived nine lives in his short time here. I thank him for the example he set, his irrepressible spirit, and his wild enthusiasm for life. I know that he is with me now. I feel goosebumps as I write this—a confirmation that he is present. He has inspired me to live as joyfully as I can, following my Inner Compass and taking inspired action. I look around me at my life and feel incredibly blessed—a far cry from those days of burnout and depletion. Life isn't perfect, but it feels good more often than not.

My Soul's mission is to contribute to others, to serve by helping them find joy while living from my Inner Space of joy first. This shapes everything that I do and all that I am. It is a powerful motivation and inspiration to keep meditating and turn inwards to feel my Inner Compass and hear my soul's calling. It is from this space of Being that I can follow the inspiration and creative ideas that keep calling me forward, expanding that mission.

My soul always knew my mission, even when I didn't. It has called me through all my challenging life experiences, knowing that each experience would unveil a deeper level of understanding to serve others more powerfully. To find my Ikigai. To live an Inspired Life. To live from the *Inside Out*.

If you could live your irrepressible life, what would you do? What is your spirit calling you towards? How can you take one small step towards that today?

In summary, the keys to tuning into your Inner Compass and activating the Miracle Modes which light up the path to everything you want in life are:

1. Figure out what *depletes* you and do less of that.

2. Figure out what *replenishes* you and do more of that.

3. Figure out what *lights you up*, and get going with that.

4. *Meditate!* It's the magic foundation of everything else.

If you would like to dive deeper into the practice of tuning into your Inner Wisdom, you can check out the free guided meditations at _www.emmagray.net_

ABOUT THE AUTHOR

EMMA GRAY

EMMA GRAY is a Clinical Psychologist and Master Coach, founder of *The Miracle Modes to Master Your Life* TM and *Business Alchemy for Women* TM programs, empowering women to create transformational change and live their Highest Purpose.

Emma is an author, speaker, trainer, and facilitates coaching programs and wellbeing retreats. Her meditations have been accessed across the globe. Wellbeing Magazine affirmed that she offers a "safe tranquil space...to open the mind...like a warm hug welcoming you home."

Join her beautiful community of like-minded souls exploring mindfulness, meditation, spirituality and self-care

www.facebook.com/groups/mindfulnesssanctuaryforwomen.

Emma lives with her family on Sydney's Northern Beaches, soaking up the sunshine and salty sea air.

Connect with Emma here:

Website: www.emmagray.net

Free Meditations: www.emmagray.net

Email: emma@emmagray.net

ALDWYN ALTUNEY

PAVING THE WAY FOR A NEW AWAKENED CIVILIZATION

Tuning into divine guidance

*W*ith my eyes closed, while I was lying down on my yoga mat during a quantum DMT breathwork and meditation experience on the Gold Coast recently, I saw visions of my ancestors and those who have come before me. I couldn't see all their faces; however, I recognised their souls.

Tears of gratitude and curiosity streamed down my cheeks as I considered what they had gone through to pave the way for me to be born.

I saw a mystical purple haze-like sensation of light flickers flowing towards the right part of my brain, with the message to embrace my feminine side and nurture myself so I could shine brighter for those around me.

Coming out of that experience, I was so inspired to take life to the next level that I created a new Facebook group titled 'Conscious Community Global'.

The group was created to support each other in raising global consciousness to quantum critical mass. One open heart is 5000 times more powerful than a closed mind! It's about being present and loving life regardless of what's happening in the world. This is a space for people to share inspiring photos, quotes, videos and other conscious media to pave the way for a new awakened civilization and potentially save lives.

The group attracted more than 200 members in 12 hours and is growing organically due to high engagement.

This is an example of me tapping into my intuition and divine guidance to birth a new group, bringing together conscious communities globally to work together for the greater good.

It has taken me some work to get to this point because for most of my life, I have come from my headspace with decisions, not the heart.

I Grew up Feeling Depressed & Invisible

Born in 1974, I grew up in a loving household of Greek, Turkish and Ukrainian heritage. As all three countries have been at war over the previous century, I jokingly call myself the 'love child' now!

Growing up on Sydney's northern beaches watching hours and hours of mainly negative mainstream news at home, I grew up angry and depressed with the state of the world. I felt invisible and that I didn't belong here for many years. I also felt hopeless and helpless to do anything about it.

I remember one night, after watching the news in our house in North Balgowlah, I was so disturbed by what I saw. I cried my eyes out and went up to my dad and asked: "Why are people so cruel? Why is the world like this?" He hugged me and said: "Darling, that's just how the world is."

For a long time, I believed him.

I soon found plenty of evidence in my life of the cruelty I saw daily in the news. My innocence was lost at the age of six on my first and last family trip to Turkey. I befriended a beautiful big sheep at my grandma's house, which I later witnessed being killed in front of me.

What I wasn't told and wouldn't have understood as a 6-year-old is that what happened was a Greek orthodox tradition that when family members come from a long way away, they sacrifice a sheep as an offering to God and to feed the poor people in the village.

When I returned to North Balgowlah Public School that year, I was bullied by fellow students. They picked on me because of my name, the food I took to school and the clothes I wore. Anything they could pick on, they did.

At a young age, my dad said to me that 'anger is danger' and I internalised my anger for years, which led to depression.

When he introduced me to table tennis, I found an outlet to release my anger through the sport and developed a killer forehand smash. Soon, I became the number one ranked Australian junior table tennis player and toured Australia and internationally for more than six years.

Not feeling like I belonged anywhere, I began rebelling at a young age and ran away from home at 13.

At age 15, my dad was fed up with my constant rebellion. When I arrived home around 5am the morning after a Halloween party, he kicked me out of the house. That day, I moved into a crazy household in Manly with a drug-addicted drummer, his alcoholic mother and drug-dealing sister.

It was a complete party house with non-stop music and jamming until sunrise each morning. After six months of this, with my boyfriend lying and cheating, the final straw was seeing my best friend at the time kissing and cuddling my boyfriend on our bed. I called my mum in tears and she graciously invited me to 'come home'. My dad gave me another chance and I ended up studying very hard alongside my brother.

I had gone from Dux of North Balgowlah Primary School to failing everything in Year 11 at Mosman High School. I changed schools at the start of Year 12 to Forest High School, which was another turning point in my life. I discovered 'the grass is not always greener on the other side' and started to appreciate my parents and family much more. I ended up qualifying to do a Bachelor of Arts in Communication (Media) degree at the University of Canberra (UC) from 1992 to 1994.

In Canberra, I met my first true love - a man I thought I would be together with for life. He was four years older than me, a creative artist and sculptor. We got along famously and soon moved in together.

While at uni, the role of Editor of the university newspaper, CUrio, became available. I applied three times before I was offered the position. I took the fortnightly publication from 24 pages to 48 pages and had 30 contributors, which I coordinated.

I became the longest-serving editor at the paper and loved the power the media had to affect change in the community. I found the media was a great way to share my voice on what I felt were injustices in the world and ways to help make it a better place to live. I wrote a story about anti-duck shooting, with the headline 'Go and Get Ducked!' and about issues that moved me somehow, including battery farming of chickens, female circumcision and stories about protecting the environment.

By the time I graduated from university, I had received High Distinctions in my majors of TV Production and Photojournalism.

I was very ambitious and did not like the icy cold weather in Canberra so my boyfriend and I moved to Brisbane in 1995. I began looking for work as a graphic designer. I soon secured casual and part-time jobs as a graphic designer, reporter for Rave, Time Off and Artika publications, market researcher, photographer and telemarketer.

Growing up with the belief that I had to work hard for my money, I was working crazy hours and my boyfriend of 4 years, by then, kept politely asking me to spend more time with him. Again and again, he asked. Repeatedly, I ignored him until one night, when I arrived home around 5am after a photography gig, he jumped out of bed half asleep.

A tall, strong man, he pushed me against the wall in a psycho hypnotic state, strangled me and almost killed me. When I eventually broke free of his hold on my neck, shocked and in terror again, I balled my eyes out. I was 22. He soon apologised when he came to his senses, but it was too late. I had already lost trust in him and the relationship.

Within one month, I was offered a full-time job as a Journalist at the Daily Mercury in Mackay. I left my boyfriend, as hard as it was because I loved him so much, and pursued my career.

This was the start of what ended up being a lucrative career in the media for me. I went on to work as a journalist on TV, radio and in print media across Australia and internationally. Since then, I have interviewed stars including Charlie Sheen, Jewel, Vanilla Ice, Hugh Jackman, Russell Crowe, Cyndi Lauper, Debbie Harry (Blondie), Alby Mangels and Jimmy Barnes, among others.

After two years at The Daily Mercury, I worked at the Coffs Harbour Advocate, Queensland Times in Ipswich, Satellite Newspapers in Brisbane,

Rave and Time Off in Brisbane, the Gold Coast Bulletin and Sun Community Newspapers (where I was a Journalist/ Sub Editor for five years).

In between, I did some work experience at Channel 7 and ABC TV in Brisbane and hosted radio shows at 4CRM in Mackay, 2CHY in Coffs Harbour and Life FM on the Gold Coast (now Juice 1073).

When I first moved to the Gold Coast in January 2000, I never planned to stay there. My goal was always to live in America, so I rented apartments for the first two years.

As fate would have it, I found a beautiful beachfront apartment in Main Beach to rent and gave a guy about $1000 in rent and bond money - believing him to be the owner.

It turns out he was renting and owed three weeks in rent! I could not believe someone would do that or that I fell for such a con artist!

From that moment on, I decided I would not rent anymore and bought my first house on the Gold Coast. I still live in that house I purchased in Southport after 20 years until now.

I believe in karma. What comes around goes around 10-fold — and not necessarily by the same people who rip others off or do harm! If you want great things to happen in your life, do great things for others.

Passionate about Inspiring Truth & Good News

I started my business AA Xposé Photography in 2002 on the Gold Coast after having a few small car accidents while working late nights with a photography company in Brisbane.

At the time, I was working as a journalist at the Sun Newspapers. When I left my position at the Sun, the business evolved into AA Xposé Media as people began requesting public relations work, copywriting, video, graphic design, editing and media training services.

I did my first media training workshops in 2003 and had repeated calls for more.

In 2005, I invested $7000 in my first personal development course in the Hunter Valley, NSW. To this day, 17 years later, I have invested more than $500,000 in business and marketing courses, as well as many different modalities of personal development. This has been invaluable for the growth of my business and myself and has given me great insight into the decisions I have made in life and the meaning I have given to them.

More Turning Points

I fell pregnant in 2009 and miscarried naturally after nine weeks at age 36. That was very hard emotionally and I did a few women's workshops after that to help me heal.

I have had a few near-death experiences in life, including having a peritonsillar abscess in my throat in 2014 - which flared up after emceeing for Colin Hay (lead vocalist of Men at Work who sang the famous song Down Under in 1980) at the Woodford Folk Festival on the Sunshine Coast.

This experience taught me to value my life like never before. Hundreds of Facebook condolence messages poured in and I began to shed tears of gratitude for all the wonderful people in my life. "Who would show up at my funeral if I died?" I wondered. "What kind of legacy do I want to leave? What kind of life do I want to live?" These are great questions that I often revisit and reflect on.

These are just some intense experiences on my life journey so far and each of these, I'm now so grateful for as they have shaped and defined me to be a stronger, more grateful person.

There are no accidents in life. I believe everything happens for a reason. A great question to ask with all challenges is: "How has this happened for me?"

Mass Media Mastery Program Launches Globally

In 2014, I launched an online media training program called Mass Media Mastery, where I teach people how to get free publicity and mass media exposure.

Members of my Mass Media Mastery program are from all over Australia and overseas, including the Netherlands, South Africa, the US, UK and NZ. Most of them are small business people, authors, speakers and social entrepreneurs.

I help people who have a great message, product or service to share it with the masses using online and offline media so they can build their credibility in the community, business and leave a legacy. In 2021, I also launched Free Publicity Secrets and Social Media Masterclasses.

As someone who has struggled with depression and had four friends commit suicide by the age of 45, I am passionate about promoting more positive news stories in the media to help reduce depression and suicide rates worldwide and lift people's spirits. In line with this, I founded a worldwide Good News Day on August 8, 2018, and the monthly Global Good News Challenge in June 2020.

Big Award Win

In late 2021, I won the national Bx award for the Print, Media and Photography category from a field of 8 finalists where I was the only female! This was a great honour, particularly as a woman in a male-dominated industry. It shows the divine feminine is rising and is what will bring healing to the planet. My business has tripled through Covid and will continue to grow as I stay true to my mission of inspiring more truth and good news in the media to reduce depression and suicide rates and lift the consciousness on the planet.

I believe a 'person on a mission has no competition' and there is an abundance of opportunity for everyone.

Advocate for Animals

As a highly empathic person, I have always had an affinity with animals.

After years of seeing animal cruelty and feeling helpless to do anything about it, I founded the world's first Animal Action Day in 2007 to raise awareness, appreciation and respect for animals. I have since run 15 annual events, raising millions of dollars worth of free publicity for different animal charities each year.

Moving from Head to Heart and Gut

Throughout my 20-year-plus career as a journalist, I embraced a very strong masculine energy to survive in the male-dominated field. I became used to coming from a determined 'head space' with decisions I made and the pressures of the job to meet constant 'deadlines' or timeframes, as I now like to refer to it.

My dad's beliefs also rubbed off on me, which were: "Use your logic more than your heart because your logic never tricks you, whereas your heart can."

I have realised later in life how important it is to tap into the heart and gut as well as the head and to have all three energy centres align. The more I trust my gut and inner guidance and tune into myself through meditation, yoga and breathwork, the more life flows. The more I'm guided by my intuition, the more I live an inspired life. The more I slow down, the more I speed up!

Love is in the Air

I had commitment and intimacy issues with men for years, ever since my boyfriend strangled me at 22. I've had this attitude that I don't need men for anything and I'll be just fine on my own! After seven years of doing 'part-time' relationships, friends with benefits, lovers, etc., I took time out to go within. I meditated, did yoga, women's circles and inner healing, including a plant medicine journey, and realised I was carrying a lot of ancestral trauma. Once I had cleared that, with new insight and more balance in all areas of my life than I had before, I finally committed to a man again in January 2022. I'm 48, he's 47, and now we're talking babies! It's still possible. Let's see... if it's meant to be, it will be!

I'm happy with him and happy in my own skin without him too. Together though, we create magic. So grateful for that. Here's to more love and fewer wars in the world - however that looks for you.

My dad is 84 and mum is 78. They have been married for 52 years and are still very much in love. As they have had many health challenges, I realise the fragility of life and how important it is to make time for family and loved ones, no matter how busy business gets!

I think it is important that women trust their intuition and bring love to what they do. For women to be empowered, they need to be open to receiving and allowing success and love in their lives without guilt. I can now say I have finally done that. At the same time, I feel the journey has only just begun!

My Ancestors are With Me

I feel a strong drive and support for what I do from my ancestors. Scientifically, it is proven that we carry the DNA of 14 generations. My great grandparents were two of the 30,000 Kulaks executed by Stalin's men in

Ukraine in the early 1930s. They were hanged outside their house on their farm in Kyiv (aka Kiev) as part of the mass eradication of Kulaks as a class.

My grandfather was in a different part of Ukraine at the time and began to speak out about it until his friends told him: "Because you're speaking out against the government, they're coming to kill you now." He then ran away to Turkey and met my dad's mum, who was Greek.

I know my ancestors are supporting me spiritually in helping others to stand up in life and speak their truth.

Future Goals

I would love to have an offline studio TV show one day - to complement my online shows on the Media Queen TV channel on YouTube. I love interviewing people and sharing their stories and wisdom. I would also like to start a global movement of more conscious good news stories in the mass media than bad news stories. I believe this will make a massive difference in reducing depression and suicide rates worldwide.

I am passionate about inspiring a positive world where people are optimistic and excited about their lives; a world where people love what they do and are excited about living life to its fullest potential. I want people to embrace and appreciate the miracle they are as human beings.

Just by being born, they have beaten about one billion other swimmers to the finish line!

Every person is a miracle and has a unique gift and message to bring to the world. I want to inspire people to recognise and appreciate their gifts, to speak up and speak out about what they are passionate about and for them to create a ripple effect of change by being courageous and speaking their truth honestly and with integrity.

The few who run the world want people to live small lives and be slaves to the system.

Many people are brainwashed by the mainstream media, education and political system and don't realise they are being brainwashed. I want people to wake up as individuals and combine forces with other 'awake people' in the community to affect positive change in the world - particularly in the areas of health, peace, sustainability and environmental protection.

"Question everything!" is my motto.

"Be the change you want to see in the world," Gandhi said.

And I say: "Shine bright and light up all those around you."

Here's to your success! May you always make the most of every moment in this precious life and live an inspired life that you and your loved ones will be proud of.

ABOUT THE AUTHOR

ALDWYN ALTUNEY

Known as the Media Queen, ALDWYN ALTUNEY is a photojournalist with 38 years' experience in TV, radio, print and online media. Aldwyn hosts Media Queen TV – Inspiring Truth and Good News on YouTube.

Born in Sydney and based on the Gold Coast since 2000, Aldwyn runs AA Xposé Media, which offers public relations, photography and videography services plus the worldwide Mass Media Mastery training program.

Passionate about raising awareness, appreciation and respect for animals, she founded the world's first Animal Action Day in 2007 and has run 15 annual events, raising millions of dollars' worth of free publicity for animal charities.

Passionate about promoting more good news stories in the mass media to help decrease depression and suicide rates worldwide and lift people's spirits, Aldwyn founded a Global Good News Day on August 8, 2018, and the monthly Global Good News Challenge in June 2020.

Meetup groups she has run since 2018 are Mass Media Tribe and The Gold Coast Business Laughter Club. She has featured in 15 inspiring compilation books, many of which are international best-sellers, and has interviewed stars including Charlie Sheen, Hugh Jackman, Russell Crowe and Cyndi Lauper.

Connect with Adwyn here:

For all socials and connection call links: www.linktr.ee/aldwyn

Freebie: Clarity Connection Call to move from being the world's best kept secret to being a media star. Book here: www.linktr.ee/aldwyn

JUSTINA CASUARINA

CHOOSING JOY - FOLLOWING THE MAGIC

Captivated by the majesty of this place—divine light dancing on water, penetrating the depths of my being, my very essence transformed. Floating in this water body, my senses are fully awakened; I feel completely in love, at home, and oh so abundant. It's just me, enjoying the most exquisite nature. Drinking in the essence of the water lilies and this moment, knowing I get to start my day at this divine lake, crafting the rest of it as I choose, joy and gratitude fill me. I take a snapshot overview of my life. I live in a most beautiful home surrounded by nature that I had only once dreamed of living in. I have two gorgeous children, blessed with one of each variety. My work is soulful, in service to the divine feminine and the great awakening on our planet, and I structure it in the way that best suits me. I live close to incredible beaches, dance regularly, enjoy the most beautiful connections with my animal companions, am loved, seen, and accepted by a precious community of wonderful humans, and I am deeply in love with the man I have always longed to bring into my life. This is me now, in my late forties, edging 50.

If I had been told this is how my life would be as a child, I would have been thrilled. However, it was a journey to cultivate living this way.

The Early Picture

I was born and raised in the suburbs, an hour south of Melbourne. I went to a catholic school, attended church on Sundays, and ate McDonald's and fish and chips once a week, along with meat and 3 veg meals most nights. I had two loving parents, a brother and sister, two cats and a dog, clean clothes, and a warm, tidy home. Always. What we didn't have, ever it seemed, was much money (especially once my parents separated). Although I felt content with life at the time, I also longed for more. When I put my requests in for things, I often didn't get them or would need to settle for the cheaper alternative. I was generally met with, "We can't afford that", or "We don't have much money," as a regular mantra, along with "oh, I wish ``, or "In your dreams" whenever I would share my desires of living an abundant and extraordinary life.

It was cold for a good part of each year growing up in Melbourne. I longed and dreamed of holidays in warmer climates, travelling, and one day living further north, in a lovely two-storey home, growing my hair long, owning a big dog, hitting the beach most days, and singing and dancing when I wanted (dance lessons were not allowed for me growing up, and I was frequently growled at for singing... apparently, I was too loud/expressive). So I just did life, my way, as much as I could.

I had a deep love for and connection to children, becoming an early childhood educator at 19. I delved deep into the healing arts young, drinking this in, and experienced an expansive spiritual awakening around 22. Life really began shifting rapidly from then on. For that, I am truly grateful. I began to see and live from a very different perspective, a place of magic and synchronicities, consciously cultivating more of these, celebrating wins along the way, (I had to really work hard at that one as I began to realise that I, in fact, was creating life in conjunction with the universe / the divine, as I went along.

I travelled the world a lot between the ages of 20 and 24, visiting many exotic and fabulous locations, and living out some of my childhood dreams.

Of Starlight & Magic

When I was called to return home to Melbourne, I had no idea why. What I did know was to follow my guidance and intuition, and it said very clearly to head home. I was right on cue as that very night I arrived back, I cuddled up with my dear soul sister and talked about storytelling, inspiring, and weaving magic into the hearts of beautiful children all over the world. That was the night Fairy Starlight, my beloved alter ego, was born.

As I have a playful, effervescent nature, loving the realms of magic, it seemed perfect. That, along with being an early childhood educator and the fact that I had let go of my previous work to follow my joy, travelling with my best friend, not knowing what was next. During that time, I was clearly intending to magnetise work into my life that acknowledged me more professionally and financially, and that allowed me to sing, dance, and be more fully expressed. I, therefore, knew instantaneously that this was meant for me. All of this, coupled with the full-body YES sensations, giggles, and extreme joy I was experiencing with my fairy sister, Fairy Bubbles, made it clear that there could be no doubt—this was the path I was to take. Onwards I went, with no business nor theatrical experience, yet a huge love for following my heart, trusting the joy this whole idea brought to me, as well as the magic and synchronicities of life.

I truly adored my time as Fairy Starlight; it was a great honour, privilege, and pleasure. I had many incredible opportunities to entertain: from huge audiences at large festivals, smaller childcare settings, to birthday parties, with many other magical characters I got to play out along the way. It was my love, joy, and mission, to "Help people to believe in themselves, their dreams, and the magic of life, whilst inspiring them to access their most full potential." This continued as a massive focus in my world until the next chapter of my life was birthed, and the support structures required for this entertainment business to continue to grow and thrive, unfortunately, just didn't come together.

I Became a Mother - An Extremely Divine Blessing With Many Challenges

I always wanted to be a mother. And after beginning my studies in the realms of spiritual midwifery, I soon had the blessing of pregnancy upon me. I was 28, initiated into motherhood in the most exquisite way, with a beautiful home birth, approximately 6.5 hours in length, in front of a roaring fire, surrounded by wise gum trees. Blessed, I was with an absolutely perfect baby girl who filled my heart and soul with endless joy. My daughter meant everything to me, and my romantic and somewhat naive perspective on love helped perpetuate a dysfunctional and tumultuous relationship with her father for many years to come. We had little support and housing stability, but my daughter and I had each other.

I did what I could to keep my dreams alive. I chose to travel every year when it was just my daughter and I, from the wintery Victorian weather to northern skies, and was on the lookout for a place where I could lay my roots in the ground, to raise and educate her. I knew it required a greater sense of community, a much warmer climate which would allow us to be outside in nature more, swimming the majority of the year, and last but certainly not least, have many opportunities to dance!

My love of music and dance kept calling me as I would breastfeed my darling girl with a soundtrack playing. During these moments, I'd see and feel my body moving in ways I had never moved before, and my desire to make that my lived experience increased. Apprehensively yet excitedly, at 31 years of age, I applied to pursue my passion for dance and, to my delight, was accepted into the Northern Rivers Conservatorium of Music and Dance. So we relocated, and there, in Lismore, I danced four days a week, minimum. If my daughter wanted to, I would bring her with me; otherwise, she was happily learning to socialise at nearby care some of the time. It was good for her. She was very easy, really, and happy to come along for the ride wherever my heart led us. We were an amazing team.

The biggest and best surprise of my life came when my son entered this earthly plane in the water, in the home he was conceived in. We thought I was having a girl! A perfect birth, surrounded by softness, love, and laughter. I was over the moon to now be gifted a son. The three of us had a lot of fun! There, in my early 30s, I wanted more than anything to provide the best for my children—organic food and other experiences. Yet, unfortunately, money continued to be an obstacle.

You see, I chose to prioritise being as available and as present as possible for my children's upbringing. Working online wasn't a thing back then. I wanted to be the mother who was always available and there for my children. When they were sick, before and after school, to give them breakfast, pack their lunches, put dinner on the table, as well as support and encourage their full expression with extracurricular activities, even if that stretched me financially.

As time went on with my 2 children, either on my hip, breast, in my arms, on my lap, in bed with me, or by my side, it became clearer and clearer that I was and would continue to be walking the solo parenting path. I was far beyond impressed with that; I went there with less grace than I would have liked, and, in truth, was deeply hurt that we weren't made a priority by their father. I was outraged that he continued to live his life however he pleased. Barely contributed a cent to support them and basically swanned in and out whenever he chose. I was and still am a romantic, a lover of and believer in love, so in those younger naive days, I hoped that things would shift. I wanted to believe what their father told me, that he was working for us all and deeply faithful, even though I could feel he was doing neither of these things. My intuitive nature was tested hugely in this relationship, and no matter which way I looked at it, I was alone with my kids, 24/7. The best remedy for those big and ongoing feelings relating to the relationship and parenting situation was to fall more deeply in love with my children and the gift of being their mother. Enjoy as much as I could of every given moment, as I knew they would grow in the blink of an eye. I was extremely devoted to and very much in love with them both. I felt endlessly blessed to be their mother.

Although being a mother has been one of the most, if not, the most joyous blessings I have been gifted with this lifetime, I have also found it exceptionally challenging. Some examples of this are: not having enough money to make ends meet, doing EVERYTHING myself for them and me without any regular, consistent support, and numerous incidents of overwhelm, stress, and exhaustion from general juggling and managing the children, the home, their education and wellbeing. Finding homes and other places to stay when homeless, holding presence and space for the children and their needs after episodes of abuse from their father when I was barely hanging in there myself, with only friends on the phone offering support, little to no time and space for myself, and of course, the endless disrupted sleepless nights.

There were times when I literally did not think I was capable of keeping going, let alone living a joyous, abundant life.

Despite my exhaustion, somehow, I managed. I became an opportunist and developed a knack for finding creative ways to make things happen, literally, even when I could have easily given up. Praying to spirit / the divine / the universe for support, guidance, and help, keeping fit and healthy, eating as well as I could, drinking the best water I could, filling my cup with the love of myself, my children, that of nature, and of course, immersing myself in dance and the jade goddess / feminine vitality practices, (which I now teach far and wide), as much as I possibly could.

Choosing joy was and still is the thing I orientate towards, always having something percolating that excites & delights me to look forward to, as well as experiencing joy for no particular reason. It fuels my days, so I never go too low.

Being in joy puts us in flow! This I know, and it has been shown to me clearly over and over again. Go where the love is, where you are celebrated. At times, for me, what would fill me is purely being with my children.

Definition Creates Reality

If one views themself in a particular way, e.g.: this is how I was born and bred, and this is how it will stay, then that is how their life will play out.

Yet what I have learnt along my life's path is that we are all expressions of the divine, and we can cultivate a life that truly lights us up.

If I chose to keep seeing myself as a poor, struggling single mother without any family support, one who had experienced domestic violence, was ostracised from her family due to a hideous assault from her older brother, had numerous incidents of homelessness with 2 children, and our beloved cat—I would have spiralled into a severe depression, could easily have given up all hope of a joyful, abundant existence, and definitely settled for things being "good enough," when they most definitely could be improved.

Being In The Right Place At The Right Time

For me, the key is continuing to dream and becoming more aware. I have written things down, consciously focused on the feeling I will experience being in the reality of actually having and receiving what I'm calling in, giving thanks for it as if it's already present in my life, speaking it into reality, and/or sometimes just having a passing thought of it.

It doesn't have to be all of the above. Sometimes just a quick intention. Other times, when it is something I so dearly wish for in my heart, I may spend a few minutes daily, possibly numerous times a day, to simply anchor this reality or the end result I am calling to me into existence.

Then, when I am introduced to the gorgeous heart-centred American man who makes me feel at home and smile, or walk into the house I have been calling in, or hear about the passive income platform that almost sounds too good to be true where I make money whilst I sleep, I KNOW I am in the right place at the right time. And you will too!

Why? Because the feeling is familiar. Everything feels right. There is a draw, an intrigue, a magnetic pull towards the person, job, home, or situation you have desired. Perhaps even the sensation of goose or "truth" bumps will be present.

Being in the right place at the right time definitely comes from flexing the trust muscle. Trusting in yourself to "know," trusting the universe to have your back, that it's working to support your greatest desires, your highest path, your personal growth, and being willing to jump in with a BIG YES when the synchronicities appear.

I Never Stopped Learning - Becoming An Expert In My Field

Basically, I kept choosing to follow my joy, studying whatever lit me up, and set my soul on fire as much as I could with my children and responsibilities. I developed 2 bodies of work based on dance and movement. The first, Spirit Dancing, for feminine embodiment. And the second, Birth Dance, to prepare women for childbirth. I studied conscious relating and sacred sexuality before immersing myself in a practice that cultivates deep self-love, helping women to know themselves intimately, heal, and heighten their pleasure pathways. It's the Embodied Psycho-Sexual Method and is based on the sacred and ancient jade egg teachings. This, along with educating people on menstrual health and awareness, led me to become a leader in my field, and to this day, 13 odd years later, I continue to practice as well as serve women throughout Australia and globally with these tools. I am blessed that I no longer trade time for money.

Alternate Income Streams To Support & Ignite Joy & Prosperity

Throughout my parenting journey, I was endlessly aware of how money could have created far more support for my children and I. I kept visualising passive income and financial ease, literally making money whilst I sleep. These intentions, I believe, helped open me to doors of opportunities in the emerging blockchain world. Through this, I have created a lifestyle where tapping into alternative income streams of legacy wealth creation is supporting and will continue to support me long into the future. In fact, legacy wealth generation is well and truly here, and I embrace and celebrate it. For myself, my children, my children's children, and beyond. I believe we are at a point in history where this is particularly crucial as the world is changing so rapidly; we cannot be certain what is coming, whether our jobs will still exist in the future, and so forth.

I didn't know what the passive income I dreamt of would look like. I just connected with the feeling of joy and freedom that it would bring me. Knowing that by embracing this in my life, I would be supported more fully to do and be all I am here to be.

How Can You Create Your Inspired Life?

- Keep dreaming, focusing on the end result / the outcome you want

- Say YES to opportunities and take action when they present

- Know when a full-body YES comes your way that it's time to act

- Stay awake to the signs and synchronicities, embracing them when they appear

- We always have a choice on how to view things/ the perception we decide to take, make a decision whether you will live a life with a half-empty or half-full cup

- Choose to focus on joy and cultivate more of this in your life

- Count your blessings, and more blessings will come ie: adopt an attitude of gratitude

- Keep choosing to move from love over fear

- Ask, "what would love do?'

- Celebrate the wins, AND....

- No matter what life presents, a great focus is keeping your vibration and frequency high, imagining the life you want BEFORE you are actually physically having it as your lived experience; then you will recognise it more easily when it appears.

Our time is limited on this earth, dear soul. How long for precisely we never know until our exiting moment. Let's make the most of this amazing and magical journey called life. With this in mind, I fill my days with joy and gratitude as much as I possibly can because challenges come and go; that is a given. It's how we navigate and view these things that is potent. This is where the magic and mastery of existence lies.

If I can go from being a girl who didn't understand her magnificence, in fact, thought that she was very average, if even that, suffering a major eating disorder that spanned over a decade, without much access to bringing her dreams into reality - to a woman who is empowered, deciding the lifestyle she wishes to live, going for it and claiming it when alignment comes, and the signs and synchronicities appear, living a life of great abundance, joy, and prosperity, then so can you!

Keep flexing the muscles of gratitude for what is, choosing an orientation toward joy, consciously creating that which you would love to experience, and letting go and allowing the magic of life to weave its wondrous ways into your world.

ABOUT THE AUTHOR

JUSTINA CASUARINA

JUSTINA CASUARINA a is a women's educator, focusing on feminine embodiment, sexual sovereignty, menstrual awareness, peri-menopause and beyond. With over 25 years' experience, she specialises in Jade Eggs and their teachings, for women's pelvic and sexual health and vitality.

Justina is a leading expert in women's psycho-sexual health & healing, a best-selling author, featured on numerous podcasts and at conferences throughout Australia. She is known for speaking the unspoken and bringing fresh new perspectives to light. Justina created Cultivating Lifelong Pleasure, Embodiment & Feminine Vitality, to support women of all ages to have empowering practices they can carry throughout their entire lifetime.

Justina holds a vision of a world where women carrying shame and guilt in their bodies is a thing of the past. She supports a new norm of women coming home to themselves, holding great love within, seeing their bodies as the sacred temples that they are. She knows that as women do this, men and children will too, creating profound transformation on the planet.

Mother of two, 20 & 16 years, Justina lives in Byron Bay Australia and is often found swimming or dancing somewhere fabulous.

Connect with Justina here:

Website: www.femininevitality.com

Freebie: www.femininevitality/offer

All socials: https://linktr.ee/Femininevitality

PART V

WELCOMING PROSPERITY

TONYA RUTTER

EMBODYING MONEY IS LOVE FOR WEALTH AND PROSPERITY

I was being strangled at work...

...or, at least it felt like I was being strangled at work.

This sensation of being strangled kept happening on and off for months. Then one day, in addition to the sense of something being wrapped around my throat, I felt like I was nine months pregnant and about to give birth, experiencing contractions and movement. One of my colleagues asked me if I was okay, to which I replied, "No! I'm not okay. I'm about ready to give birth to a ghost baby!" I had no idea what was going on with me, so I called a friend who is also a medium.

My friend's response was, "Well, I see a woman with long blond hair, dressed in an 1800s prairie style. She looks notably pregnant, like maybe around nine months, and...Oh my God! She's being strangled!"

It turned out this woman had been murdered about 200 years before. She wanted acknowledgement of what had happened to her, plus she was letting me know that I had an ability that, up until that moment, had been hidden from me. Soon after, I had people who died from accidents, illness, and suicide coming to me, letting me know what happened and why. Some people had recently departed; others had been dead for years.

Not long after the initial death experience, I began experiencing how the living died in past lives as well. These experiences were highly visceral. I saw.

I heard. And even felt everything that the person went through from different viewpoints – as the victim, the perpetrator, and the omniscient view as a spectator – moving simultaneously from viewpoint to viewpoint.

One notable experience was a General who was shot in the stomach with a cannonball. I could see a huge black hole in my stomach and felt like I'd been cleaved in two. My abdominal aortic artery seemed to expand while my heart pounded and got bigger from the pushback of the arterial blood. My body shook and kept alternating between hot and cold, while it felt as if my abdominal aortic artery and heart both exploded from the pressure. I really thought I was going to die during that experience.

Another experience was a man who died in a fire. I gasped for breath, but it was as if the oxygen had been sucked out of the air. I could feel myself suffocating and began to pass out.

I also felt every bit of a man impaled through the throat, which I could feel and taste warm blood rush down my throat and into my chest. And without knocking at death's door, I know how it feels to die from being stabbed with a sword, with a knife, and with a bayonet; how it feels to be shot with a gun and shot with an arrow; even how it feels to be hung by both suicide and murder. I know what goes through a person's mind when they die by drowning, both accidental and purposeful. I know what both the body and mind feel when being eviscerated, crushed, or suffering a drug overdose. I know how quickly a person dies from a broken neck in an accident or a broken neck in an attack. I know the fear that strikes a person during a heart attack, asphyxiation, or being strangled by hands or rope. Going through these experiences wasn't what I'd call 'fun', but they did help me as an author.

Over the years, my energy practice has evolved from being a past life expert to having the ability to travel through someone's DNA and accessing memories from their childhood, previous lives, and ancestral memories passed down to them. Our memories result from electromagnetic charges of thoughts and emotions held within the cells. These electromagnetic charges create our background programming that we often don't realize is there. Yet, this background programming can affect us by sending out a frequency the Universe matches for things we may not want. I work within these electromagnetic charges by moving through space and time, jumping timelines from the past, present, and future, dissolving unwanted electromagnetics, and changing background programming to reflect what is wanted. This ability is what I use to help clients with their money issues, health issues, and relationship issues.

A few years ago, I was frustrated with my own money issues. Life was not going as I had hoped. My business was on hiatus while I figured out what direction to take, as I moved away from health coaching. Bills were coming in, and foreclosure was only a payment away. Even though the income from my job was decent, it seemed like there was always something that would come up that needed money to be fixed. One stressful day while rain lashed at the windows and the wind howled, I sat at my office desk and, in desperation, called out, "Please, money, come to me!"

And... Money answered.

Even though my windows were closed, a gust of wind blew around me, and I could feel an energy enter my body. I sat there, amazed and dumbfounded, as my body tingled and an otherworldly electricity raced along my skin. Then Money spoke to me, and I realized money is more than just an energy; it is a Goddess. She told me her energies are of graciousness, giving, and love. She wants to be shared for the betterment of mankind. She wants us to be vessels for her, so she can spread love throughout the world. This completely altered my perception of what money actually is. Prior to this, I hadn't thought of money as having a heartbeat or being a living entity, or even having a mind of its own. Prior to this, money was merely an energetic tool.

Not long after my encounter with Money, I had a conversation with a fellow coach about her money issues. I could see, hear, and feel a pulse coming out of her heart and instantly knew this was her Money Pulse. There was a break at the top wave of the pulse, and thus began my journey of helping people heal their Money Pulses.

Since that first encounter with the Money Pulse, I've come to understand it more. I have seen Money Pulses that are strong, broken, weakened, moving backward, blocked, or even upside down. Every living being with a heartbeat has a Money Pulse. Money is the same frequency as love and is attached to the heart. In essence, Money is Love. As long as you follow your heart, you're also following the money. The question is, are you blocking your Money Pulse?

Back at the beginning of 2020, I had a nudge to travel and experience the world. However, I had no clue how I could do that. Not to mention that, at that time, there was this thing called COVID going around, which made travel impossible. But I also knew that, at some point, the world would open up again. I knew I would have to quit my job and work in my business full-time, but there was a lot of fear surrounding the idea of quitting my job; such as fear of not making enough money in my business, fear of failing in my business, and shame over being a failure and, let's face it, being a loser. I also felt a lot of responsibility towards my career and thought there'd be no way they could function without me. (Hello, ego!) My youngest was 18 at the time and still lived at home. She has a number of health issues, and my excuse was that I couldn't leave her to her own devices. I was afraid she wouldn't be able to take care of herself. I waffled back and forth with selling the house and even spoke to a realtor about it. Apparently, the timing wasn't right, though, because I received none of the paperwork the realtor sent me!

Early in 2021, that nudge became more of a push. I considered selling my house, keeping my house as a base for the business, or giving the house to my daughter. I kept waffling back and forth between those three ideas. My daughter got tired of hearing me talk about the subject. The idea of quitting my job still scared me shitless, not to mention abandoning my daughter and being a BAD MOM. In addition, I was afraid that I'd lose the house if my business wasn't successful. I was afraid my daughter would hate me if I lost the house and we became homeless. I was afraid my family would be ashamed of me if I lost the house and we became homeless. I was afraid of losing my clients' respect if I lost the house and we became homeless. Notice the pattern here? I was afraid of not having a base, someplace permanent that I could call home. The deeper issue, however, was fear of stepping into my own power because of so many limiting beliefs such as "I'm not good enough," "I can't do this," and "I'm just a failure."

Fear after fear after fear held me hostage so that I couldn't move forward. Instead, I became complacent in my desires, thinking I was doing tasks to move me forward when actually those tasks were meaningless busywork. My rational mind tricked me into thinking that I was being productive in my goals. Cue the shock when I realized I was actually hiding away because doing something new, while exciting, was freaking scary! When I realized this, I wondered what happened to the fearless girl who jumped off of a 100-

foot bridge (and led a number of inebriated adults to do the same) and dreamt of bungee jumping and skydiving. Where did that girl go?

In the spring of 2021, I had a vision of a crocodile-filled lake with a tree on each end of the lake, and between the trees was a vine. In the middle of that vine, hanging on for dear life, was me. I did not want to let go for fear of falling into the lake of crocodiles and being eaten alive. I realized the vine represented all my fears, and the crocodiles represented the unknown. I was holding on to my fears, because in my rational mind, those fears were keeping me safe.

After a few deep breaths, I let go of the vine and fell screaming into the lake while a crocodile dove in after me. The crocodile swam under me, catching me. I landed on its back. It swam to shore, climbed out, and deposited me on the ground. The crocodile – that big, scary unknown – was my safety net. I had nothing to fear. As I came to this realization, a giant bubble welled up from deep within my solar plexus, rose upward, and shot out of me.

A deep-seated fear I didn't even realize was there had left.

After this, I decided to sell my house, quit my job, and move out of the country. I wrote a letter of resignation with a working end date. Even though I didn't turn that letter in, I still wrote it with the thought, intention, and energy of turning it in. Boy, was that an anxiety-ridden letter to write! My heart raced, my breathing was uneven, and it even took me a few tries to write it. Nonetheless, I did it, and that created a new creation cycle of events. I contacted an agent and started getting my house ready to sell.

My house was officially listed on the market in August, and the sale was finalized in November. I still had that resignation letter from months ago and remembered the fear and anxiety when writing it. This time, however, there was no fear of writing out my actual resignation letter. Instead, I felt free. I felt whole and had a gut-load of excitement. My heart was leading me down this path. I knew that no matter what, I would be fine, and my daughter would be fine. I quit my job, moved my daughter into an apartment, and moved to Mexico in mid-December. My daughter has learned how to take care of herself and has gained immeasurable confidence and independence since living on her own.

Downsizing from a 3-bedroom home with a 2-car garage plus a separate workshop to two suitcases was an exercise in freedom. I had to choose what to take with me, what to give away, and what to throw away. At some point, I'll be taking off again to another country and will be, once again, downsizing to a backpack and a bag.

As I got ready to move and began letting go of material things, I shed plenty of energetic layers to get down to the 'real' me: *Who am I? What do I do? How do I contribute to society?* Since I moved to Mexico, I've proudly claimed my identity: I am Tonya Rutter, Master of Energy, Witch and High Priestess, and I claim my identity without shame, without blame, and without guilt – but with strength, passion, and purpose. Wealth is abundant with the freedom to be me and not apologize for who I am or what I do.

Back when I first started my energy practice some 13 years ago, I was disconnected from the money aspect. Like many other energy practitioners, I spent a few years simply navigating the changes happening in my life, honing my abilities, and discovering who I was throughout the process.

Once I became serious about turning my energy practice into a business, the phrase "Money is Energy" came up time and time again and how there must be an exchange of energy, i.e., payment in exchange for services, in order for the recipient to have a full experiential experience; otherwise, they don't receive the full benefit as it was meant to be accepted. The problem was that I wasn't actually charging for my services – this is something very common, especially among energy practitioners – due to the belief that my abilities were gifts and, therefore, not a chargeable service. I was in such a lack mindset that those were the types of clients I was attracting – people who didn't want to pay or didn't have the funds to pay. Over time, I came to understand this more. Then I heard that "Money is Love." Again, while I intellectually agreed with the statement, I didn't understand it, nor did I feel it. I wasn't fully embodying that statement.

Embodying Money is Love means fully feeling it. The energies of money are Graciousness, Giving, and Love. The frequency of money is the same frequency as love. As spiritual beings, we are the creators of our realities. We create money, meaning we, ourselves, are money. I am money, and you are money. There is no separation between ourselves and money. If I love myself, then I must love money. Yet, many people have a hard time saying, "I love money." However, embodying "Money is Love" is what leads to wealth.

When we think of wealth, oftentimes, our minds immediately go to money as wealth. However, Wealth is a State of Being. Being wealthy means I have a healthy body, healthy relationships, and abundant money in the bank. Wealth also means being happy and fulfilled with my life, with what I do, what I create, who I interact with, and how I contribute to society at large. Being wealthy also means feeling joy, contentment, and excitement by simply walking out my front door and going to the local market.

A simple exercise to begin the path of embodying Money is Love is to exchange the word "money" with the word "love." Instead of creating money transactions, you're creating love transactions. You're not doing something for money; you're doing it for love. How often do you hear someone talk about a program or business venture and say, "...but I'm not doing this for the money." That statement alone pushes money away because if it's not being done for money, then it's not being done for love, so what is it being done for? Unless it's being done for both purpose and money, emptiness sets in. As you begin to equate money with love more and more, you'll start embodying Money is Love. You'll begin to see there really is no separation between money and love, allowing you to live from a life of wealth.

I am living life and experiencing how it feels, not simply going through the motions. There are so many more experiences I want to have, and I will. Consider that a year ago, being homeless terrified me, and now I relish not having a permanent home! A year ago, the thought of leaving my daughter left me feeling panicked, but now she has confidence and is independent, living on her own! A year ago, I had so many limiting beliefs about my business, but now I'm busier than ever! My office is the world – it's wherever I happen to be at any given moment.

Before, I was a spectator in my own life, standing on the sidelines, waiting for something to happen. Now, I'm the participant, leading the charge, allowing the energies of life's joys to move through me and experiencing them fully. Being free in this way has brought wealth and abundance to me. This doesn't mean you must shuck your material possessions in order to be happy and free. It simply means allowing yourself to let go of the things keeping you small. And as for me, letting go of my home is what allowed me to spread my wings. But for others, having a home base may be what allows them to fly.

Shedding the layers of guilt, shame, and worthlessness, along with all of the negative "I" statements such as: "I can't," "I'm not good enough or 'smart enough' or 'rich enough' or just not enough,"; getting down to the core of who you are and being that person without shame, without guilt, without apology, and without blame, allows wealth, abundance, and prosperity to flow to and through you. Dissolving the electromagnetics and background programming holding you back is critical in your journey to creating the life you desire. When you become a Master of Energy, you become a Master of Yourself, which means nothing has power over you; even those negative "I" statements suddenly become a thing of the past.

If this chapter resonated with you and you are curious to take a deeper dive into your negative "I" statements and discover what electromagnetics need to be dissolved, you can book a Money Pulse Assessment with me. But for the meantime, I encourage you to start embodying Money is Love as you begin to change your money story for wealth and prosperity.

ABOUT THE AUTHOR

TONYA RUTTER

TONYA RUTTER is the founder of Tonya Rutter Coaching, Nyx House Media LLC, Nyx House Ventures LLC, and Nyx House Press. She empowers heart-centered creatives, coaches, entrepreneurs, executives, and intuitives into Becoming Limitless, by showing them how to tap into the magic they have within themselves for abundance in their businesses, careers, wealth, relationships, and health.

Tonya's specialty involves helping clients with money issues. She assesses their Money Pulses by taking a deep energetic dive into their DNA, thought patterns, beliefs, and upbringing, to access memories and background programming keeping clients from moving forward.

Tonya has been featured in Passion Vista Magazine's *Women To Look Up To In 2022*. She is an Executive Contributor for *Brainz Magazine*, a si*STAR* with *Team Manifest*, a member of *The International Society of Female Professionals*, has been interviewed on numerous podcasts, and enjoys writing steamy, dark urban fantasy.

Tonya enjoys spending time under a moonlit night, or curled up with a good book and a glass of wine, or writing the sequel to her book, *Blood Promise*, under the pen name Tonya Kerrigan.

Connect with Tonya here:

Website: https://tonyarutter.com/

Free Gift: https://tonyarutter.com/431-2/

For all socials and a Money Pulse assessment:
https://linktr.ee/nyxhousemediallc

ANGELIQUE PELLEGRINO

SHOULD I STAY OR SHOULD I GO?

Most of us, women, are healers in some way or another… so we often end up with someone we want to heal; this is unconscious yet a big part of our default programming.

So when this gorgeous guy with a charisma second to none told me early in our relationship that he did drugs occasionally, I thought, "no big deal! He won't feel like having any when he's with me. I will help him give it up and heal him." This is a thought typical of the empath—who feels they can take everyone's burden away.

Little did I know what he meant, as I was awfully naïve. The main thing was that while I was with him, we would never have any money. He would always get his drugs first and then gamble. He was a master hassler, pushing and forcing his way until he got the money, which often came before paying rent or buying food.

I'd never heard of mental illnesses before, never alone the terms "narcissist" or "bipolar." Yet, all these words have been mentioned to describe my late husband. So that you know, I disagree with them all as no one can fit in a box: everyone is so different and unique. So even though I dislike labels because they, more often than not, project this label to be real even if it wasn't the case, they do provide a point of reference that most people understand.

In between drug sessions, he was kind, generous, very funny, very wise, really knew people well, was a great chef, and a great dad to his daughter and son. So I chose to believe that money was not as important as love, and it was an opportunity for me to dig deeper and become more resourceful. I also knew that the Universe has an endless supply available to us and all I had to do was be open to receiving.

I didn't mind that he didn't have any material possessions like a house, car, and all that comes with that because I knew the power of the mind. I knew he/we could create anything with our great minds. And, rest assured, the ideas were plentiful. But no matter what he tried, he failed epically. It even got to the point where I thought that some old Italian mamma had cursed him...

Love conquers all, right? As complete opposites: he was the street kid, and I was the bookworm—we were madly in love. Nothing was more important to him than the children and me.

Navigating through life is tough enough for everyone with regular jobs, but try adding on the demands his habits caused... Wow! That was a massive challenge; I won't deny it. The worst part was always the time leading up to his fix because he'd become aggressive until the session was over, and then he'd be a little lamb again for a while.

Over time, I managed to put more space between events for him, but he still never worked, and I never got to take it away completely.

Yes, many others would have given up many times over, and I allowed myself to contemplate the idea when he made me take out all our money from the bank in 2000 because the world was going to end. He gambled the whole away, but I thought of the repercussions and weighed out the pros and cons.

It's a fine line, and no one can decide for you as all circumstances are different. For example, this woman in Brisbane who left her husband was picking up her kids from school one day, and as they all sat in the car ready to go home, the car burst into flames, and they all died. Of course, it was the husband who thought "If I can't have them, no one else will'

I am not saying that my husband would have done that but what if? He was Italian, after all, Sicilian.

But I didn't stay out of fear. I became fascinated with psychology and all healing modalities. As you know, the purpose of psychology is to understand why a person does something so that you can then work on healing and change.

Seven years into my marriage, the answer finally came: He had been raped by an uncle when he was only 11 years old, week in week out, for far too long. Let me tell you the story as he told me.

His mum and dad had emigrated from Italy. Dad was working three jobs to support his family and his three stepbrothers, who had just arrived in the country. And because mum was cooking and cleaning for five adult males, she didn't see what was happening under her eyes either...

Every so often, the entire family would come together for Sunday lunch. Pasta making was in action, music and wine were flowing, and people were playing cards, smoking, drinking, dancing, and singing; no one ever wondered why little Johnny would hide in his bedroom. He was thought of as being the 'black sheep'.

One day his Uncle X, who had established a barbershop, said to him, "Hey Johnny, you walk past my barbershop every day after school. Why don't you come in and help me tidy up, and I will give you a few shillings." So he did and brought the money to his mum to help with the food.

As Johnny looked up to his uncle a lot as a father figure because his dad was never home, he listened to him. They talked about a lot of things, and he even gave him some sexual education. All of this led to him touching him, fondling him—saying, "don't worry, I would never hurt you" and one day— BANG!

OMG!

Then when mum and dad would go grocery shopping on a Saturday, Uncle X would turn up and give it to him over the blue bathtub... If his dad ever found out, he would have killed his stepbrother, and Mum would have been left alone.

See where I learnt to think of the repercussions. I couldn't sleep for a week after discovering the root cause of his issue. I wanted to go and kill the uncle myself or at least tell everyone in the family—who thought he was such a goodie two-shoes—who he really was: a pedophile. Then we wondered how many others he had touched.

So, in reality, when my late husband would have a session, it was all about releasing that pain that kept lingering in him 24/7. He would go into a trance for up to 16 hours... And I will keep the rest private, but you can imagine.

So my Quest was to Heal Him.

He was such a beautiful man inside out. When I told people that my late husband was shooting up drugs, they immediately assumed it was heroin. But no, it was cocaine. Yes, BIG difference. You see, the first one is a physical addiction that leaves you in a calm stupor, while the other is a mental addiction connected to superior sexual activity. So I decided to step out of my boundaries to provide him with, let's just say, more creative sex so that he would heal.

He was f***ed up! He was like a battered Woolf that needed recovering...

He knew that he would be in great danger without me, so he hung on to me like dear life. And I knew that, but I had big shoulders, and I knew that even if I left him, I would attract the same type of relationship if I didn't learn all my lessons here. I also knew that it was my karmic experience and that I had chosen this path before coming here to use as a point of contrast.

Let's face it. You can't have it all good all the time simply because we live in a world of duality. No plane would be able to fly, and no door would close if we didn't have opposite polarities. There will always be ebb and flow. The idea is to learn to surf with it.

Again, I have seen time and time again that women leave their husbands or partners only to find themselves soon after with the same type of man with the same problems. It was a recurring pattern.

Instead of fighting the situation, which would have been useless, I focused on my quest to heal him. I knew that by working on myself, I would lift him. I did this in many ways. For examples:

- He didn't want me to work as he didn't trust himself to be alone, so I saw that as an opportunity to get creative in any way I wished. For example, I designed a range of children's wear that I sold through party plans. See, abundance comes in many ways.

- I did a degree in interior designing, which came in handy as we moved a lot. LOL!

- My main focus was to be happy, so I played with my children—a lot. I taught them to use their imagination. I taught them to cook and clean. I taught them that our life is like a speck in the ocean, so tiny and short in comparison to the universe's immensity. There's no time to waste holding grudges and being grumpy; focus instead on having as many wonderful experiences as you can.

- I meditated as much as I felt like it to help me stay anchored.

- I became attuned to Reiki and used it on him daily.

- I read all about the law of attraction and implement it every day.

I read countless books on personal development. Later on, I even studied psychology to become a Counselor, only to understand where the medical system was at to build a bridge between spirituality and psychology in hopes of finding a fast solution to heal his trauma.

The secret to my successful marriage to an extraordinary man who was very ill came down to one simple fact: I really focused and understood and lived *the power of now*. I constantly let go of the past and the future. I was really embedded in the 'now,' appreciative of all my blessings.

Despite all my studies and best efforts, I did not succeed in restoring him, but that was not our contract. All I could do was give him a safe haven with lots of love. Music was also a great tool to keep our vibrations high.

Usually, hurt people hurt others. Well, not my Johnny. He was, in fact, super protective of us. Many would see this as controlling, but it made me feel safe. In truth, I already knew then about the disappearance of women and children. So, what I loved about him was that he was determined not to pass on his diss-ease to anyone else.

Unfortunately, I took him to the water many times, but he did not want to drink... This taught me that you have to accept the things you cannot change. It was his journey, not mine.

Today, 13 years after his passing from cancer, I wish he was still around, and I had been able to bring him back to life. He was my best friend; he was always the light of a party. His charisma was second-to-none. In fact, every woman who ever met him fell for him... Oh yes, everyone. And the funny part is that most of them thought they'd be a better partner to him than me. LOL.

You see: his vice was not to be with other women; it was his relationship with the needle.

Two years after his passing, I went to a healing fest. At one point, a lady was offering a talk to those who had recently lost someone, so of course, I went. I asked her why I didn't feel my husband more as we were so deeply connected before his passing, and she replied, "He's right here, kneeling in front of you with red roses. He is saying thank you for not giving up on him. He is saying that he had done what he wanted to do on the planet, and it was time to let me go..."

I cried like a baby, of course, but was somewhat relieved to hear that.

After endless work on myself, I now know on a profound level that:

1. We create everything ourselves, the good and the bad, with our vibrations which derive from our thoughts... what we choose to believe.

2. We need contrast to learn and grow from because we live in a world of duality.

3. When someone does drugs to the level he did, they allow unseen and unpleasant identities into their body. Not only do they create havoc but they are hard to get rid off.

4. There's often a big gap between men and women because men who are meant to play the field before they settle down have been desensitized so women need to learn to stretch their boundaries to meet them at least half-way.

5. The mind will do exactly what it thinks we want. Always!

6. We have truly endless abundance available to us now. The only reason we cannot feel it, touch it or smell it is because we're not letting it in.

7. Trust the law of karma

8. Let go... Let go... Let go... All day long... of everything.

9. When you fall in love with someone you never know what they have shoved deep into their subconscious to forget. You don't know how it will affect their lives and yours but one thing is for sure: if they don't deal with it, it will come to the surface in explosions and create pain for all concerned.

10. Keep pumping positivity as there is a turning point. Never give up!

11. The secrets lie in our subconscious so work on releasing what no longer serves you to empower you.

My 20 years of marriage were a whirlwind of pleasure and pain which has taught me a lot and makes me a truly unique Healer and Teacher today. No university degree could teach me the level of understanding I have. Having watched my beloved husband battle the way he did between his levels of pleasure and pain made me determined to find a way to heal people deeply all over the world as fast as possible, so they don't have to suffer for years as he and I did.

This is where I learnt the true meaning of the serenity prayer:

"God, grant me the serenity to accept the things I cannot change, courage to change the things I can, and wisdom to know the difference."

Unfortunately, the solutions to his healing did not align with me while he was still alive, but I truly believe that I have them now. I am passionate about sharing them to heal the planet so that we can all live a life we love, just as I do now.

Whether you are feeling useless in the healing of a loved one or useless because of some other endeavor that doesn't work the way you want it to work, I suggest that you love yourself for doing what you do and accept that this is no longer your journey.

You never own anyone. You just get to be part of their life for a while, and you will reunite later on a different plane. So let go... Let go of your attachments and need to control, having to be right, the need to be strong, the need to be busy—Let it all go.

You don't need to forget the person or the issue when you let go; you just detach yourself from the situation. Go within. Realign yourself with your center, your source, and milk that feeling.

Every time you exhale, you let go of more and more... Try doing that all day long for a week and see what happens. Keep letting go while in a meeting. Keep letting go while talking to someone else on the phone. Keep letting go while on the toilet. Keep letting go while driving. Keep letting go while doing the dishes.

Isn't life wonderful?

Abundance Comes in so Many Ways.

Keep your ears and eyes open—Don't miss any opportunity.

Here are a few ways abundance comes in:

- Someone buys you coffee
- " does your make-up or hair for you
- " finds some money on the ground
- " gives you some clothes or something else
- " cleans your garden for you
- " puts the bins out for you
- You discover an upmarket fashion label dress in a second-hand shop
- You win the lottery
- You get a pay rise or promotion
- You receive a privilege or upgrade of any kind for free
- You enjoy the profit of a sale

The list goes on. The important thing is to recognise it and see it for what it is when it comes in. Then, milk the moment, the energy, as this will produce more of it. It's truly magical.

It truly works. Today, 13 years after my husband's death, I have finally cleared my vibrations from the traumatic 20 year-experience and its ripple effects. Our family is thriving. Both of my adult children have found their special person, have blossoming businesses, are fit and healthy due to the choices they make, and even gave me my first grandchild. She's already blowing our minds at eight months of age. Imagine what's coming...

And even when challenged, daily, we focus on the solutions to stay on the divine path, and more good things come in. We, actually, often think of something, and it just appears. Things seem to fall into place amazingly well. And because we remember that all is temporary, we really relish every minute, and I invite you to do the same.

You've got this!

You are so much more powerful than you realise...

Allow more to come in...

Let go now and just be.

ABOUT THE AUTHOR

ANGELIQUE PELLEGRINO

ANGELIQUE PELLEGRINO, known as The Angelic Transformer, is the founder of Be OMG! Mentoring.

She helps men and women over 30 who are in emotional pain to have rapid, permanent and powerful results in transforming their lives. She does this through only one to three sessions of RTT (Rapid Transformational Therapy), which embraces several healing modalities including hypnosis to manifest phenomenal results.

Angelique is passionate about taking people from pain to pleasure and seeing women live lives they love by permanently removing trauma from their subconscious.

Born in Switzerland in 1957, she travelled the world extensively before settling in Australia. She has studied many healing modalities to build a bridge between spirituality and psychology. She found counselling too past focused, reiki healing too slow and life coaching too future focused. In RTT, she found the perfect methodology. It provides a proven solution for fast and phenomenal transformation. Angelique can do sessions via zoom or in person in her Brisbane studio.

Connect with Angelique here:

Website: https://angeliquepellegrino.com/

Linktree: https://linktr.ee/AngeliquePellegrino

DR. VIRGINIA LEBLANC (DOCV)

FREEDOM IS CALLING

THINK WITHOUT A BOX

*W*hat is inspiration, and where does it come from? What does it mean to live an inspired life? Many of us do not come from a family, culture, religion, or other environments that speak of such a thing as "inspired living," nor have the means to live from a place of inspiration that ignites joyful living. Or do we?

I recall the beginning of my "or do we" journey in 2010... I was feeling uninspired and discontent in the workplace and had begun my entrepreneurial journey. I was discussing with a colleague my difficulty putting what I did into words: helping clients navigate life or career transition by looking inward to define their path by shifting perspective and pivoting into new joy-filled realities. Eventually, intuition whispered into my ear—Creative Life Design (CLD). CLD is based on the internal guided process fueled by inspiration with creativity at center led by intuition. That field remained relatively unknown, until the inspired living movement (living life on individual terms as its value proposition and main message).

The Creative Process

In 2016, as I sat to write 'Love the Skin YOU'RE In: How To Conquer Life Through Divergent Thinking,' I came across a quote by Pam Leo that spoke to my soul: "Let's raise children who won't have to recover from their childhood." I used it as the opening quote to the chapter "Train Up a Child:

The Creative Process," followed by the opening message, "Dear Society, train your child to be who they are, not what you want them to be. We all have a purpose. It's on us to find it."

How we view the world is influenced by how we come into and exist in it. Most people never truly live, let alone discover and walk in their purpose. The cares of life easily distract and lead us astray, intentionally or unintentionally. Those cares start with our caregivers and transference of their conditioning and limiting beliefs, producing replicas.

Children are not meant to be clones. Life is about discovery. It's a creative process where each person must discover their own truth and path. Picture the child coloring outside the lines of a design. While the creative process is not void of structure, for that child the limitations of structure do not exist and are in the mind's eye (intuition). Why do we not seek to understand the source? Conditioning teaches that there is only one perspective: to assume the child lacks the capability or understanding. The child is never asked "why" they did so (only admonished). What if we allowed the child to test budding gifts through exploration, self-discovery, and divergent thinking with the absence of boxed-in thinking that causes identity crisis and fear of self and others? Worrying about children "not" being like everyone else will cause them to be like everyone else rather than themselves.

The methods by which we measure and condition children ignore the essence of individuality and abandon the creative flow in life. If you train a child in the way they should be (loving the skin they're in), that child will not depart from that path. They may go off your expected script while discovering life. It's okay. Give them foundational structures like respect with freedom. Allow them to think without a box, and they will stand for themselves and others in a purpose-driven life.

Adulting Revelations

One of the greatest revelations as an adult is coming into the conscious realization that we do not know what we do not know and that it IS okay. What matters is the response to that aha moment as well as the answer to the question, "What are you going to do about it?" (fight or flight). Tap into your childlike intrigue and exploration, or continue to color inside the lines?

Most people color inside the lines to cover up the lack and fear of imposter syndrome. I was one of those individuals. I put on masks that manifested in innumerable negative, self-sabotaging ways that stifled possibilities because I was not conscious of any other way. I had long since abandoned my childhood inner voice, my intuition, for the love of being normal to avoid the pains of life. What I didn't realize is that it's all a part of the journey and that our pain leads to soul purpose.

One of the greatest tragedies in life is unrealized human potential because of the inability to understand and respect pain. Our home and school training teach us to avoid pain by doing xyz, giving a false sense of security. Meanwhile, the universally accepted training method for our young centers around societal expectations and uniformity **when we were meant to be originals, not copies. We were meant to live inspired and be anything but normal,** yet constructs are set up, and we strive for normalcy, ignoring and shutting out our guiding inner voice for a half-hearted, pain-filled, uninspired life. So many of us miss our calling because of socio-cultural conditioning and associated fears of deviating from the "norm." Who defines normal? And why do we hold ourselves to standards we did not set for ourselves?

As collective members, we want to be part of something bigger than ourselves. But that often leads to allowing oneself to diminish and suppress individuality to fit a mole instead of charting your course. Be the captain of your fate and the master of your soul. Yes, there is a weight that comes with doing so, but there is also freedom and joy in moving outside your comfort zone and sitting in uncomfortableness. The trick? Embrace fear and it will become your ally. Realize you carry innate, unique value as an individual, evidenced by employing intuition to walk out your soul purpose.

Understanding Purpose

Purpose is more than a trendy term, concept, or in-vogue thing. It is our reason for being that lives in the soul. Societal messaging mutes the true notion being the reason for which something exists or is made, as a replacement or interchangeably for its competitive action form: to set as an aim, intent, or goal for oneself). There is a significant difference, and understanding it is key to inspiration.

Understanding the charge of "soul" purpose, that it is no respecter of person or background and our reason for being, is the first step toward empowerment and living an inspired life of creative design. It requires seekers to shed limiting "less than" skin to be "more than," working contrary to norming constructs that lead us down conditioned paths into hierarchies, caste systems and classes.

Admittedly, we make routine choices every day, but who/what is leading those choices? Is life leading you, or are you leading it? We usually do not consciously consider or find the answers to these questions until we find ourselves in the boxing ring facing fears that activate preservation instincts. That inner voice (intuition) reintroduces itself, giving choices: retreat, remain and accept consequences, or fight. In this conscious intuitive place, we move closer to soul purpose, the gatekeeper of our path to inspired living.

The competition, the inner battle with self (the soul), will continue until you exit the box and walk in your soul purpose. If you lead your life by intuition, you will ignite true joy and arrive at the ability to be your own boss in mind-body-soul and achieve inspired, sustainable wins.

Think Without A Box

For most of my life, I did not intrinsically trust my intuition and played tug of war instead of following the flow. I ignored synchronicities because I was thinking with a box, blocking joy and prosperity in my life due to limiting beliefs. I was not truly leaning into my internal director...that entity that leads and guides us into all understanding...that does not consciously come from us (call it intuition, source, spirit, God). I worked my way outside the box, but the box was still in view, and it was debilitating because it contained my issues with abandonment, acceptance, security, and so on. It was not until personal work in my 30s that I realized the box was meant to keep me in, out, or hovering about in futility. With that revelation, I began to break free.

I grew up poor to modest means in the south Texas box: an environment where there was little to no inspiration; money was the thing parents worked hard for and the thing that prevented them from tapping into the flow of life. My early years were mostly happy; I was raised in the country and too young to fully understand struggles. Yet so, by age five, I had already learned important lessons about faith, hope, love, fear, absence, loss, and innocence.

Inspired living was not on the radar, and never a conversation around a dinner table. Mom worked hard to keep food on the table, a roof over our heads, and a car to get us from point A to B. She was busy trying to manage her reality and provide a better life than the one she was living. My father sacrificed his calling to work in the oil field for the family and drank to dull pains and deal with lack. Nonetheless, inspired living was in my soul and kept pulling throughout life.

One would think by leading major initiatives, climbing the ladder, and excelling in everything I touched in assignments with Joint Forces commands at the Pentagon and Department of the Navy, Booz Allen Hamilton, Indiana University, and the National Pan-Hellenic Council that I was operating in my soul purpose. I was not. I was performing on purpose, simply surviving. Even though outside the box, I was still endeared and blocked by it, suppressing my calling. When I came into that conscious fact, I was able to change the game.

Conscious Intuition

Our intuition is constantly speaking, but the noise of life dims its voice from the conscious. Looking back, I recall an early experience with conscious intuition as I played in my room, jumping on my bed. Inside my closet doors, I heard a rattling. My curiosity was piqued, so I jumped down to inspect. As I reached for the rattle, a voice stopped me, prompting me to ask my parents if I could play with my new rattle toy. I had never asked permission to play with my toys before. Why did I this time? They immediately knew what the rattle was, and mom kept me from returning to my room while daddy grabbed a shovel and chopped off the head of the rattlesnake.

Intuition is innate as a child and always in play because of unlearned behaviors and fears; there are no boxes. Adulting under the confines of conditioned expectations presents difficulty escaping the box. The only way to is through conscious intuition, the process starting in the subconscious that brings information, solutions, and understanding on how to proceed into the conscious, unconditioned mind. By abandoning the box, the power behind conscious intuition—divergent thinking—has way. Divergent Thinking is the ability to integrate messaging from intuition, without apparent deliberation, through the faculties whereby hunches are generated by the unconscious mind rapidly sifting through past experiences and cumulative knowledge for creative-analytical problem solutions. Bringing intuition into consciousness breaks the chains of conformity to think and be like others because it is unique to you. It is your corner woman and has the power to overcome the noise preventing you from hearing and answering your soul purpose.

Take the "Great Resignation" between 2020-2022, which resulted from a lack of workplace joy and workers moving into a space of conscious intuition. Once conditioned blinders came off that opportunities do exist outside normal conditioning, reactions were swift and decisive to abandon ship.

Finding Individuality in the Collective

What all of this comes down to is the inherent collective conflict between societal constructs and individuality—your free will and expression of the true you. The primary question: how does an individual thrive and find success in a collective? The problem: The "American Dream" and promise envisioned. We are sold through propaganda that by following the rules and normed formula, a career ladder meant for one person at a time, we would get to that dream. Been there, done that, tried it with souvenirs, y no más gracias. This is NOT inspired living.

Transformation does not come overnight but is a journey moving from the competition with oneself into collaboration with your soul through the spirit to extricate yourself from collective fears. It wasn't until life happened in the workplace for the last time that I rediscovered that childhood companion—conscious intuition—and began to process, understand, and connect the dots to what it truly meant and looked like to live inspired; I was losing the fight. I was pursuing the American Dream, unconscious that I was allowing life to lead again: punching a clock; obeying orders to ethical dilemmas; jeopardizing my health; biting my tongue; and accepting a lesser role possessing unrivaled knowledge and know-how simply because of hierarchical constructs.

The questions: Who was I, and more importantly, who did I want to be slapped me awake. When I realized I was playing a losing game on someone else's board that I did not sign up for; when the game began to negatively affect my wellness and snuff out my soul, my perspective shifted, revealing that I was serving an incongruent, unagreeable mission.

My soul began to speak loudly with clarity and passion, igniting a decisive choice in me to stand my ground, speak truth to power, honor my oath of office, and speak up for myself and others facing injustices in the workplace. I was on a career path that I believed would deliver me to the American Dream and applaud my courage for pursuing it, particularly working for an organization touting honor, courage, and commitment as a slogan. But the organization was not honorable, courageous, or committed to do the right thing. I found myself at a crossroad and the only choice to love the skin that I was in.

Before deciding to remove myself from employment, I withstood unparalleled challenges and treatment, including attempts at constructive discharge that caused me to question my judgment, ability, expertise, and decision-making in a way never experienced in my professional career. I did not consciously realize that when playing the game according to someone else's rules, no matter the facts, being right is irrelevant and out of one's control; I was beating my head against a brick wall. Conscious intuition was the key to snap me into unconditioned reality and remind me that free will WAS in my control and the choice to abandon ship was the only choice between living or dying a slow death. The choice ignited joy, unspeakable joy in my life to live inspired.

My intuition was screaming for some time, but the deafening noise of comfort and false sense of security held my decision longer than it should have. Conscious intuition helped me find my way back to knowing my worth, realizing that I was at a crossroads with diverging paths, and the need to pivot to lead life. I leaned into my source (God) and embraced the fear of being light amid darkness, and THAT made all the difference in rediscovering my individuality and being my own boss in mind-body-soul and business.

Follow Your Flow

Conquer life by leading from the heart, mind-setting and following the flow of your conscious intuition, not emotion. Tap into that inner voice regularly for inspiration and know that it's okay to redefine and never too late. Step out in faith, discover, or rediscover your passions and develop strength in mind-body-soul. Joy, fulfillment, prosperity, wealth, and health wait for you.

You MUST abandon the box to learn how to flow and dance in the ring with life. The "how" is risky when you cannot feel the rhythm, so seek wise counsel for guidance and lived experience in next steps along your journey. Let faith, hope, self-love, and courage be your companions to shut out the noise of life and define your path.

Perspective is everything, and the box is blocking yours. Whether you are in it or outside it, you're still hovering about it. It's the reason you have not been able to find your way to inspired living. Your intuition cannot breathe. Your intuition and free will are being crowded out by fears of doubt and other subconscious limitations you may not even be aware of. Adjust your crown (perspective) and unleash the creativity inside of you. You are meant to do and be more. You were meant to be different and live inspired.

See With True Vision

The days of traditional thinking that making a lifelong career in one industry is the sign of achievement or success are long gone; don't be afraid of that. An unfortunate number of people ignore the fact that our reality can change at any time, when the only true assurance in life IS change. What to do in the face of change? TAKE ACTION.

As one diversifies a financial portfolio, to provide a greater chance of shelter from certain risk, adverse loss, or total ruin, how much more should we apply the principle of diversification to our lives? Think about it. Does it not stand to reason that diversifying your skill sets, experience, streams of income might prove a similar outcome?

The greatest gift of life is choice. The ironies are neglect of that birthright and the complexities that unfold with it. Our societies were founded on the entrepreneurial path, and it is one that allows us to exercise this gift to capacity and see with true vision to ignite joy and prosperity in our life. Have you thought about being your own boss? Don't know where to start? Great news! You've started by reading my chapter. Want to know the next steps? Consider this my invitation to visit Defining Paths (DP) virtual home at DefiningPaths.online and join our family. Our mission is transformation through transition and our passion is to help you discover and stand up in your soul purpose. My personal story became my client mission, and why I founded DP, a heart-centered, socially conscious global movement and network of thought leaders, change agents, legacy builders, and purposed entrepreneurs seeking to heal, rebuild, and transform not only their lives and online businesses from the inside out but that of others for sustainable wins in holistic wealth and profitability, i.e., inspired living.

Exercise your birthright and choose YOU. Learn to hear, know, love, trust, and lean into your intuition consciously. It will help you see with true vision because it comes from your soul. Are you defining your path, or is someone else? Perhaps you too have a quiet voice tugging at your core? Do not ignore it. If you are feeling some kind of way—frustrated, out of sorts, restless, conflicted—they are signs, synchronicities trying to pull you into understanding that you are not where you were meant to be. They are trying to disrupt the negative flow in your life (your existing condition). They are calling you to your soul purpose, inspiration, and creative flow. It is your choice whether to live abundantly and step into your greatness.

If you are a woman and you've been sitting in the background accepting the "less than" role, it's time for you to step into the light and be "more than." If you are retiring military who wants to define your own path, it's time to lead from the front; DP has your back and will stand you up in civilian life through purposed entrepreneurship. If you've already taken that leap of faith and started down the entrepreneurial path about to give up, it is our mission to help you heal, rebuild, and transform your circumstances and put YOU back in business to be your own boss in mind-body-soul and business.

When I finally answered my call to inspired living through purposed entrepreneurship, I began to see with true vision, and you CAN too. Let us help you reconcile your past so that you can rebuild your present and step into your future of possibilities, thinking without a box. Once you understand that there is a greater calling than chasing the almighty dollar, holistic prosperity will come to you by investing in people first. It really IS intuitive just like choice. Choice is NOT a luxury, it IS your birthright, and inspired living is the result of choosing the road less traveled by. Do not trade your birthright.

When you stop thinking in boxes, you WILL unleash your superpower. In fact, it is patiently waiting. My question to you: Are you ready to think without the box? Are you ready to face your fears and connect the dots to define your path? Freedom is calling. Let freedom ring through inspired living and Defining Paths!

ABOUT THE AUTHOR

DR. VIRGINIA LEBLANC (DOCV)

DocV is a respected, highly sought multidisciplinary expert and global thought leader delivering value worldwide across industries uncovering key ingredients to pivoting through career-life transitions, aptly earning her the nickname "THE Pivot Maestro."

Her story and work leading major transition efforts with Joint Forces commands at the Pentagon and Department of the Navy, Booz Allen Hamilton, Indiana University, and the National Pan-Hellenic Council led to her passion for personal wellness, development, and online business transformation, and in turn, to the founding of Defining Paths (DP), a heart-centered, socially conscious company, movement, and network with a transformation through transition mission to heal, rebuild, and transform lives and online businesses from the inside out.

As a Holistic Transformational Coach & Online Business Leader, DocV is putting YOU back in business, equipping clients to identify and take the next steps to face fears, connect the dots and think without a box to conquer life with a "be your own boss" mindset in mind-body-soul and business.

Dr. Virginia LeBlanc is the international bestselling author of *Love the Skin YOU'RE In: How to Conquer Life Through Divergent Thinking*, her autobiographical love-letter to "Society" on socio-cultural conditioning, mindsets, lessons learned, facing fears, and overcoming in life, love, and business.

Connect with DocV here:

Website: https://definingpaths.online/
Free Ebook: https://thepivotmaestro.com/nextsteps-connectingthedots-giveaway
Linktree: https://linktr.ee/definingpaths.

CINDY D CERECER

F***CKING INVINCIBLE

*I*nspiration is everywhere. Sometimes, in the most unlikely places. Upon musing over this chapter and what I would write about, the universe gave me an incredibly humbling experience. As a Colon Hydrotherapy trainer, I always tell therapists, your clients to come to you; they are mirrors and your biggest teachers.

The other day, a young man about 20 years old came into the clinic because he had been having some ongoing gut issues. I wasn't even supposed to be working (I have manifested and trained an incredible team of therapists that take care of all Colonic Care clients for me), but somehow, I ended up chatting to this lovely young man. It turns out he had an eating disorder when he was 12 (just like me), and although well on his way to recovery, he had some lingering gut issues he wanted to fix.

It was such a magical conversation because I could really empathise with the super dark, irrational, disconnected, and just downright out of touch with reality places that the eating-disordered mind takes you. It's outright bloody torture, and it's constant. It's a negative voice inside your head that has been yelling loudly at you for so long that it begins to sound like you. And then suddenly, you end up thinking it is you.

"YOU'RE DISGUSTING. YOU'RE WORTHLESS. YOU'RE A PIECE OF SHIT. YOU'LL NEVER BE GOOD ENOUGH. YOU SUCK. YOU'RE UGLY. EVERYONE KNOWS YOU'RE GROSSE. EVERYONE IS LOOKING AT YOU. EWWW, DON'T LOOK AT YOURSELF. YOU'RE HORRIBLE. YOU'RE DUMB.

YOU'RE FAT. YOU DON'T DESERVE TO EAT. ETC. ETC" ..... All day, every day.

Now that I've recovered, I can laugh at the insanity of it all now. The young man and I spent way more time than we usually allocate for a colonic consultation, laughing, swapping war stories, and marveling at the frightening similarities of our crazy journey. I told him, "I used to spend quite a bit of time in the corner of my house rocking backward and forwards, banging my head against the wall (it used to shut the thoughts up for a bit)—but ironically, at the same time—I'm a straight-A student and school captain. "AHAHAH I WAS SCHOOL CAPTAIN TOOOOOOO," he blurted out.

The connection was there, and I knew this client had come in not only for a colonic but also for a connection and alignment on a soul level. Him being 15 years younger than me, I saw there was an opportunity to share hope and inspiration that everything that life throws at us is a gift that will teach us more about ourselves than we could ever imagine.

So, I told him a story that I don't whip out very often because it's pretty dark, but in the darkness is the most mind-blowing miracle. There is a saying in Spanish that "every monster has its magic," and for me, my monster definitely changed my life forever in the most enchanting way. I knew as I shared this story with him that it was also going to be the story that I would share in my chapter ... so here it is, the story about how I became f***cking invincible.

For this story to begin, we have to go back into that corner of the room in my house, where I'd sit and bang my head against the wall. It was one of those days when my chaos was so bad that I would have done anything to make it stop. The bad news was that: Back then, several years ago, the DSM (Diagnostic and Statistical Manual for Mental Illness) had classified eating disorders as incurable. You could attempt recovery, but one could never actually recover.

The only way to truly alleviate the pain was to "top myself off." I'm using a euphemism because suicide is a very unpleasant subject, but that's where I was, trapped in a foul and excruciating place.

However, it gets even more distorted and convoluted. Thanks to my eating disorder, I hated myself so much that there was no way I would allow myself the pleasure of dying. My eating disorder decided that it would be far more painful and punishing to force myself to do something that I had no idea how to do, AND that was documented as impossible. I felt I was so horrible and pathetic that I didn't even deserve the solace of death. So my f***cked up brain decided to force myself to recover.

Cutting a very long story short, after a long and arduous journey of discovering who I truly was and tremendous personal growth, here I am a good 20 years later, and I 100%, without a doubt, consider myself fully recovered with absolutely no chance of relapsing ever. I don't care what some bullshit diagnostic manual says; I'm recovered. I know because I can feel it in total alignment in every single aspect of my being. Nevertheless, funnily enough, just out of curiosity, I looked it up a while ago online to see what the current version of the diagnostic manual said about eating disorder recovery, and apparently, it's now possible to recover. Not only did I change it for myself, but I also managed to change it for everyone else too!!

I'm immensely grateful for this experience in my life because—Now, I honestly feel like I am capable of anything. F***cking Invincible - and I have extrapolated that feeling into every single aspect of my life.

There was a myth in my family that the women were incapable of birthing naturally - due to their hips. It was genetic, and apparently, I was going to endure the same fate ... BOOM! - 4 homebirths later - all happy and successful vaginal deliveries. I was told I would never be able to breastfeed because of insufficient glandular tissue; it's a physical deformity in the makeup of the breast tissue - BOOM! - I breastfed all four kids until the age of 3; even my midwife said she had never seen anything like it before.

Now I'm not saying that achieving these things was easy, not at all. They were a tremendous slog, second only to my recovery. A daily ritual of whatever I needed to do to achieve my goals, I became slightly obsessed with personal growth, emotional release, and anything that would help me achieve my goals - but I achieved them!

So, when the thought occurred to me one day that I would like to create a life of abundance in which I am not reliant on "working" to support my family, once again, I honed in my superpower of being f***cking invincible and set out on a journey to achieve my goal.

I remember the day my husband and I decided to take the leap of faith. We had been on a juice cleanse for about seven days. We had three kids: a four-year-old, a two-year-old, and a newborn. My husband was the breadwinner and worked in IT. He's a smart man and has a well-paid job. His boss was nice, and he worked only 5 minutes from home. He had peaked. Without taking on some sort of corporate position that would require him to work crazy hours and fly interstate every couple of weeks - this was the best that things were going to get.

We had hit a glass ceiling. One that meant that we were only going to be able to take a few weeks of holiday once a year and would have to be quite budget-conscious, at least until the kids were old enough for me to go back to work. That was all well and good, but there was one more very important deciding factor: *My husband hated his job.* It involved him spending the entire day in front of a computer and sometimes coming home after the kids were already asleep.

In case you haven't done a longer juice cleanse, I highly recommend it because about day 7 is where you start to feel f***cking invincible. You feel like you've cracked the code, and if everyone on the planet could do a juice cleanse with you right now, all of the world's problems would be solved. So, around day 7, my husband decided to quit his job, and I decided to take a crack at starting my own colonic business. We wanted to make money on our terms so that we could make what we wanted and spend more time with our kids.

What we didn't realize at the time was that we had decided to become entrepreneurs. I didn't even know what that word meant, but I was hell-bent on generating as much money as I could on my terms. Did we achieve it? You bet we did, and the lessons we learnt along the way left us feeling confident and capable that we can generate our own cash flow wherever, whenever, and without compromising our values.

So how can you do it in your life too? Here are my 7 steps to achieving any goal you desire:

1. Believe you are f***cking invincible

You may have heard that the single most powerful thing anyone can do is to know oneself. BULLSHIT. As soon as you get stuck in a story about who you are any why you're no good at maths because you used to have a maths teacher that made fun of you ... blah blah blah blah blah ... you're stuck in ego and on a rant that will take you absolutely nowhere.

I'll let you in on a little secret that will save you years of spiritual mentorship and thousands of dollars on personal growth courses if you are open enough to digest it. You're not who you think you are. You're GOD. Now that may sound a little sacrilegious and possibly even upset a few people, but before you book me in for an exorcism, let's substitute the word GOD for "source."

Think about it - where did you come from? Even if you are an atheist, it's impossible to deny that there is a little bit of "secret sauce" in the creation of life. You can't just throw a whole bunch of molecules in a blender and create a person; there's that x-factor that makes it all happen, that little bit of fairy dust that puts breath into your body and sparkles in your eyes. So without this "source," you are just a pile of matter, molecules that will deteriorate back down into the earth; therefore, you must BE SOURCE.

What exactly is "source" or "God"? Well, it's just energy, but it's an extremely powerful life force with the potential to be anything it needs to be. Where thought flows, the energy goes. So, in reality, you are whatever you believe you are.

Hence why I said before that knowing oneself is useless. One must CREATE oneself, and you create yourself with your thoughts.

This is where you need to be super mindful of your thoughts around money. There are numerous negative beliefs about money. The list simply goes on and on and on ...

1. Money is the root of all evil
2. Rich people are greedy
3. You can't have your cake and eat it too
4. Money changes people
5. Money makes you stuck up
6. Too much money can be dangerous
7. It's better to be poor and happy than rich and sad
8. Money can't buy happiness

9. I don't deserve a lot of money

10. You need to be really smart to have a lot of money

11. You need to work really hard to have a lot of money

12. Waning more money is selfish and greedy

13. Money corrupts

14. You need money to make money

15. If you have a lot of money, you might lose it all

16. Money is hard to get

Honestly, this list could go on forever.

The most powerful thing I learnt from my eating disorder is that thoughts only have power over you if you let them. If you want to believe all these negative things about money ... no worries, good for you ... but you're not going to achieve financial freedom thinking negatively about money.

So I started telling myself...

1. Money makes life easier

2. Money makes the world go round

3. Money is everywhere, so it might as well be in my bank account too

4. The more money I have, the more I can share

5. I am a money magnet

6. Money is energy, and it flows to me

7. I love money, and money loves me

8. Making money is easy and fun

So every morning, wake up and tell yourself you are SOURCE, you are powerful, and you create your reality. Money is awesome, and you are F***CKING INVINCIBLE.

2. **Be extremely clear about what your goal is. What do you want? What will things look like and feel like when you achieve them?**

You have to be super clear on what your new reality is going to look like. What is it that you want to achieve? Why do you want to achieve it? What's your motivation? What's your inspiration? What will it look like to you when you achieve it? How will you feel when you achieve your goal? Write it down, imagine it, visualise it and when you achieve it, readjust and redesign new goals for yourself.

3.   Find a mentor

There's a saying; you know what you know, you know what you don't know, but you don't know what you don't know. This is so true when it comes to stepping into a frequency that you have never experienced before. This is where mentorship comes in. I would never have been able to achieve my goals in the time frame I did without someone who had already achieved them to look up to and get advice from.

When choosing a mentor, you want to find someone who has what you want. Someone where you could say, "I'll have what they're having." Mentors and coaches rapidly increase your chances and velocity for success.

I have had so many mentors and coaches over the years. Many I have paid for, and some have just fallen into my life. One of my mentors once said to me; I used to think making $10,000 a month sounded hard, then I started hanging around people who were earning $100,000 a month. That's when $10,000, all of a sudden, felt easy, and I started earning $100,000 a month too.

Start hanging around people who have what you want and start doing what they do. Once you have found a mentor that you trust and feel aligned with, If they give you advice, take it. If they tell you to jump, jump. Trust their guidance and let them direct you.

You will know you are finished with a mentor when you no longer feel aligned with their teachings. You will feel that you have learnt all that you can from this person, and it's time to move on and find the next mentor.

4.   Take daily action towards achieving your goal

So now that you know what you want, and you have a mentor to know how to get it, you will know exactly what you need to do on a daily basis to achieve it. You will have to study and dedicate time to activities that move you in the direction of your goals. Make a list of things that you need to achieve and get done. Do them. Every day. No excuses.

5. Prepare to grow, prepare to change; it's ok to let go

As you embark on your journey of daily activities to bring you closer to your goals, you will find limiting thoughts and beliefs that challenge you and make you question yourself.

You might find yourself thinking; "I've bitten off more than I can chew. I'm not smart enough for this. I don't have time for this. I'm being too ambitious. I'm delusional. I'll never achieve this goal. If only I had support from _(my partner, my parents, my friends)_ this would be so much easier."

All of the above thoughts (and probably many more) are just your old brain trying to keep you stuck. The 'poor you' trying to keep you poor. The 'fat you' trying to keep you fat. The 'sick you' trying to keep you sick. The 'depressed you' trying to keep you depressed. You'll need to power through and remind your brain that you are awesome, that you are capable, that you are powerful that you are f***cking invincible, even on days where you don't 100% feel like you are.

It's ok to let go of the 'poor you', they 'sick you,' the 'stuck you' - you're going to enjoy hanging out with the strong, empowered, confident, financially free you soooooo much better.

6. Prepare to lose friends or relationships as you shift vibration. Let them go with love

This can be a bit of a hard pill to swallow. Your circle of friends is going to change. We are the combination of the five people we hang around the most.

When I first embarked on my journey to financial freedom, I was surprised at how many of my "friends" laughed or rolled their eyes when I said: "This is who I am, and this is what I'm going to do".

I remember very clearly a conversation with one of my mentors. He makes his income online, sales, and investing. He said with a touch of sadness, "To this day, my parents think I sell drugs because they can't get their heads around how I make so much money but don't have a job."

I still like my old friends, but I don't see them as often as I used to, and yes, they are still stuck in money struggles and unable to live the life they truly desire.

My new friends are much more fun to be around as they match my vibration. We chat about projects and plans that we are working on. We share our secrets for higher productivity, we share stories of personal growth and transformation, and we celebrate each other's successes.

7.   Never ever, ever give up

This one may seem self-explanatory, but success is never a straight line. Sometimes, it's going to take more time and more failed attempts than what you initially planned. Some goals have taken me years, decades longer than I anticipated. So what? Pick yourself up, dust yourself off, readjust your compass and get right back in the ring. The game only stops when you do.

Good luck, champion - now get out there and start living your best life!

ABOUT THE AUTHOR

CINDY D CERECER

CINDY D CERECER is a mum of four and a leader in the Wholistic Wellness Community. A veteran Colon Hydrotherapist, she is the owner of Colonic Care in Melbourne, Australia and has led the way for many as a Colon Hydrotherapy Trainer and Mentor.

Cindy has also been a Certified Holistic Nutritionist, Life Coach and Theta Healer for more than a decade. She is the Principal of ICHTA (International Colon Hydrotherapy Training Academy) and the President of ICHA (International Colon Hydrotherapy Association).

Currently she is completing 4 PHD Programs in Holistic Health, Healing and Medicine at the University of Natural Health in Indianapolis.

Intuitive Living is something that Cindy is very passionate about - often known for her unconventional approach to EVERYTHING - marching to the beat of her heart and dancing to the rhythm of her soul is a non-negotiable agreement that Cindy has made with her higher self to live a life of love, learning and happiness.

Connect with Cindy here:

Website: https://coloniccare.com.au/

Email: cindy@coloniccare.com.au

Linktree: https://linktr.ee/CindyDCerecer

ABOUT HILLE HOUSE PUBLISHING

KRYSTAL HILLE founded Hille House Publishing in early 2021 in answer to the call of collaborating with thought leaders so that collectively, we can bring human consciousness to a tipping point of personal power and sovereignty.

With this fourth anthology, we have now helped over 80 thought leaders become international bestselling authors to share their stories and expertise and position themselves as leading experts on a global stage.

We will continue producing books that awaken, inspire and empower humanity into deeper sovereignty and connection and we welcome to hear from you if this is something you are also passionate about.

Krystal is also a Soul Leadership Coach and Embodiment Teacher. She helps change makers and conscious creatives to step into their zone of flow and discover the essence of soulful leadership so their passion can ignite global change.

With 30 years in leadership, a background in theatre directing and female empowerment, Krystal is a multiple international #1 bestselling author, winner of the CREA Brainz Global Business Award 2021 and host of the Soul Leadership Podcast.

Aware of her multidimensional self, pre-Covid, Krystal facilitated spiritual retreats to Egypt and ran the Temple Nights across Australia.

She holds a BA Hons in English Literature & Theatre Studies, a diploma in Life Coaching and TimeLine Therapy and is a certified Tantra Teacher and Reiki Master. She is a popular contributor to international festivals, summits and podcasts and has written two solo books and contributed to a further four anthologies.

Originally from Germany, Krystal lives with her two children in county Victoria, Australia.

If you would like to join future multi-author books or write your solo book through Hille House Publishing, connect with Krystal here:

Website: https://krystalhille.com

Email: krystal@krystalhille.com

Socials and free Inspired Living Masterclass: https://linktr.ee/krystalhille

Printed in Great Britain
by Amazon

26157393R00138